CHRISTMAS SONGS
FOR FINGERSTYLE UKULELE

Arranged by Fred Sokolow

Editorial assistance by Ronny S. Schiff

ISBN 978-1-70513-909-7

HAL•LEONARD®
7777 W. BLUEMOUND RD. P.O. BOX 13819 MILWAUKEE, WI 53213

Visit Hal Leonard Online at
www.halleonard.com

Contact us:
Hal Leonard
7777 West Bluemound Road
Milwaukee, WI 53213
Email: info@halleonard.com

In Europe, contact:
Hal Leonard Europe Limited
42 Wigmore Street
Marylebone, London, W1U 2RN
Email: info@halleonardeurope.com

In Australia, contact:
Hal Leonard Australia Pty. Ltd.
4 Lentara Court
Cheltenham, Victoria, 3192 Australia
Email: info@halleonard.com.au

INTRODUCTION

Every holiday season, the 25 songs in this collection are heard all over the world. Some of them were written more than 70 years ago, but are as well-known as any contemporary, popular songs you could name. Others were composed more recently, but seem destined to last as long as "White Christmas" or "Rudolph the Red-Nosed Reindeer."

Many were No. 1 hits when they first appeared, and all of them have been recorded by hundreds of popular artists.

Like any melodic, well-written tunes, they sound great when played on a ukulele! In these pages, the songs are presented two ways:

- A lyric sheet that has the lyrics, chord letter names, and chord grids, so you can sing and strum to accompany yourself, and...

- A fingerstyle, chord/melody arrangement that shows you how to play each song as an instrumental.

Plus, you can also sing and strum, and then play an instrumental solo in between your vocals.

Chord/melody playing is one of the most satisfying skills on the ukulele; it puts the uke on a par with piano, guitar, or any chording instrument. And it sounds wonderful when you play songs as well-written as these Christmas tunes. Playing through this collection, you'll add some favorites to your repertoire, and pick up some new pointers on how to play songs in the chord/melody style.

Merry Christmas,

All I Want for Christmas Is You

Words and Music by Mariah Carey and Walter Afanasieff

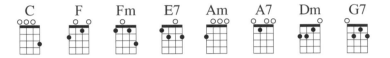

Verse 1

C
I don't want a lot for Christmas. There is just one thing I need. And
F   Fm
I don't care about the presents underneath the Christmas tree.
C
I don't need to hang my stocking there upon the fireplace.
F   Fm
Santa Claus won't make me happy with a toy on Christmas day.
C   E7   Am   Fm
I just want you for my own, more than you could ever know.
C   A7   Dm   Fm   C Am Dm G7
Make my wish come true: all I want for Christmas is you.   You, baby, oh.

Verse 2

C
I won't ask for much this Christmas. I won't even wish for snow. And
F   Fm
I just wanna keep on waiting, underneath the mistletoe.
C
I won't make a list and send it to the North Pole for Saint Nick.
F   Fm
I won't even stay awake to hear those magic reindeer click.
      C   E7   Am   Fm
'Cause I just want you here tonight, holding on to me so tight.
C   A7   Dm   Fm   C Am Dm G7
What more can I do? Baby, all I want for Christmas is you.   You, baby, oh.

```
              E7                            Am
Bridge    All the lights are shining so brightly ev'rywhere,
              E7                            Am
          And the sound of children's laughter fills the air.
              Fm                    C            Am
          And everyone is singing;    I hear those sleigh bells ringing.
              Dm
          Santa, won't you bring me the one I really need?
                       G7
          Won't you please bring my baby to me, quickly?


              C
Verse 3   I don't want a lot for Christmas. This is all I'm asking for:
              F                    Fm
          I just wanna see my baby standing right outside my door.
              C                    E7   Am                    Fm
          I just want you for my own, more than you could ever know.
              C                    A7      Dm         Fm         C
          Make my wish come true. Baby, all I want for Christmas is you.
```

All I Want for Christmas Is You

Words and Music by Mariah Carey and Walter Afanasieff

"All I Want for Christmas Is You" was co-authored in 1994 by Mariah Carey and her longtime collaborator, Walter Afanasieff, who has produced and written with a long list of famous singers. The song topped the charts in 26 countries and has become one of the best-selling singles of all time. It's the most recent addition to the holiday music genre.

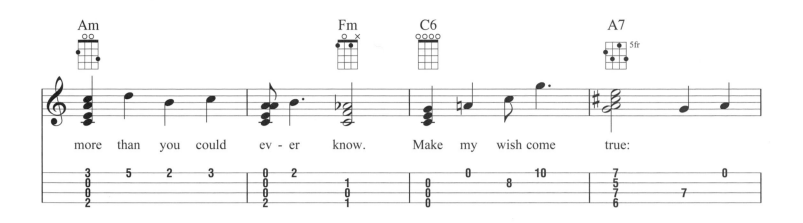

more than you could ev-er know. Make my wish come true:

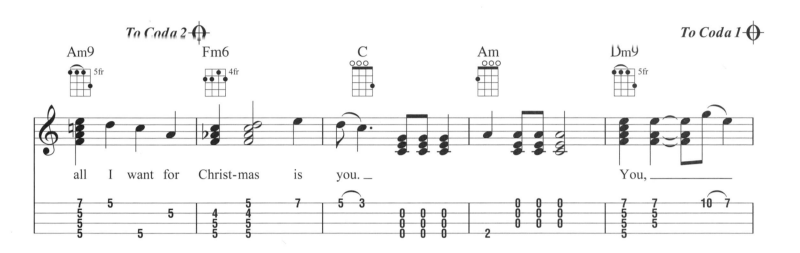

To Coda 2 ⊕

To Coda 1 ⊕

all I want for Christ-mas is you. ___ You, _____

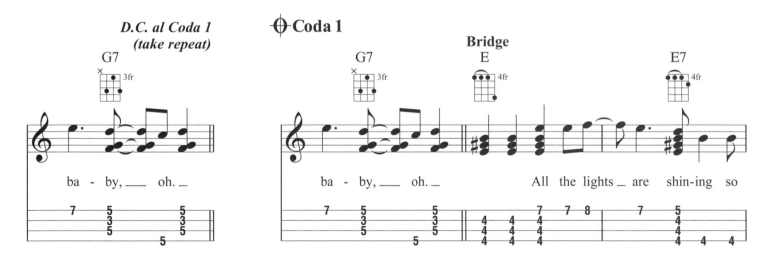

D.C. al Coda 1
(take repeat)

⊕ **Coda 1**

Bridge

ba-by, ___ oh. ___

ba-by, ___ oh. ___ All the lights _ are shin-ing so

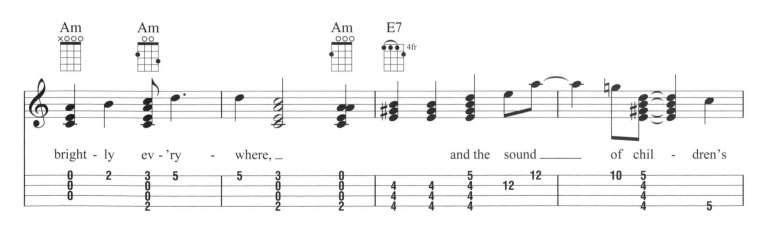

bright-ly ev-'ry - where, _ and the sound _____ of chil-dren's

laugh - ter fills the air. _____ And ev - 'ry - one _____

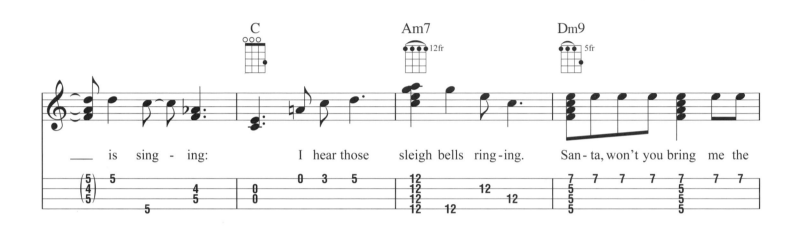

_____ is sing - ing: I hear those sleigh bells ring-ing. San - ta, won't you bring me the

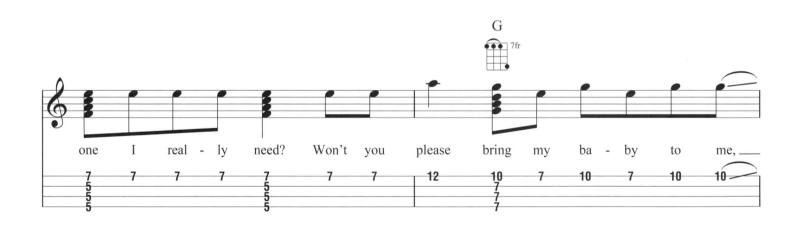

one I real - ly need? Won't you please bring my ba - by to me, _____

D.C. al Coda 2
(no repeat)

⊕ **Coda 2**

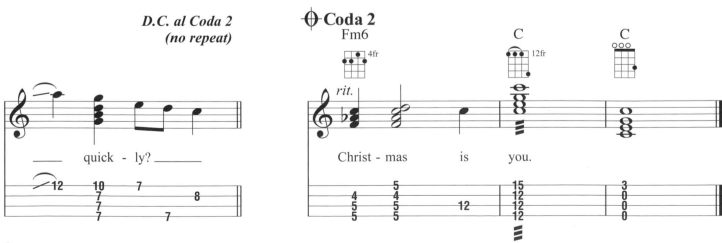

_____ quick - ly? _____ Christ - mas is you.

Blue Christmas

Words and Music by Billy Hayes and Jay Johnson

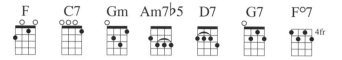

Verse 1

           F   C7
I'll have a blue Christmas without you.

       Gm   C7   F
I'll be so blue just thinking about you.

     Am7♭5   D7   Gm
Decorations of red on a green Christmas tree

G7   C7
Won't be the same, dear, if you're not here with me.

Verse 2

           F   C7
And when those blue snowflakes start falling,

       Gm C7   F
That's when those blue mem'ries start calling.

     Am7♭5 D7   Gm   F°7
You'll be doing all right with your Christmas of white,

   C7   F
But I'll have a blue, blue Christmas.

Blue Christmas

Words and Music by Billy Hayes and Jay Johnson

Most people associate "Blue Christmas" with Elvis Presley, because of his 1957 version of the tune. However, in 1950 it was a No. 1 hit on the country charts for Ernest Tubb – and first recorded in 1948 by country singer Doyle O'Dell. Elvis didn't care for the tune, and he instructed his backup singers, the Jordanaires, to come up with a backup vocal arrangement so silly that the recording would never be released. However, the Jordanaires, like Elvis, didn't know how to do a "bad" vocal, and the song topped the charts once again.

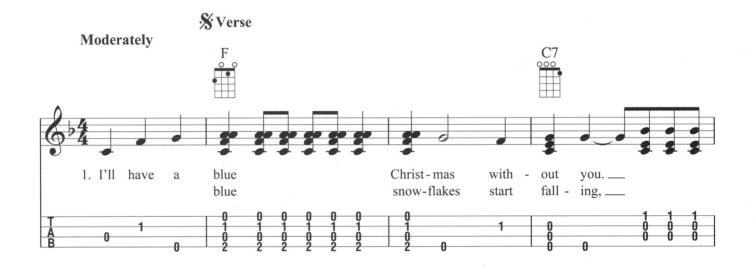

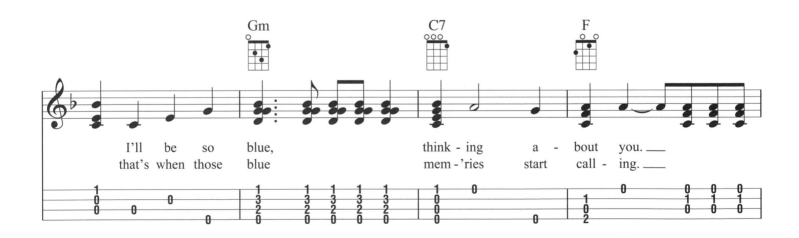

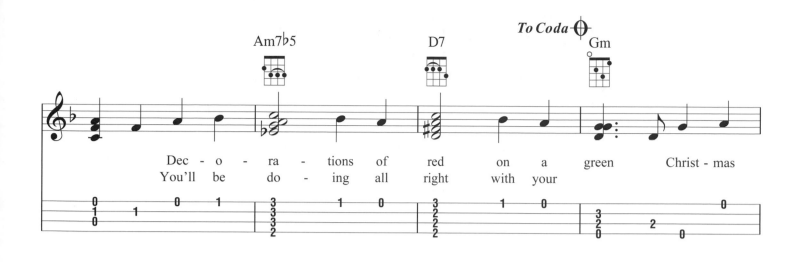

Dec - o - ra - tions of red on a green Christ - mas
You'll be do - ing all right on with your

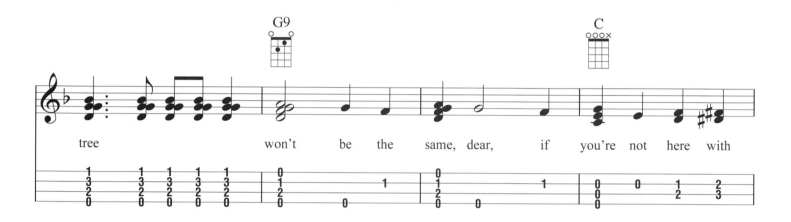

tree won't be the same, dear, if you're not here with

D.S. al Coda

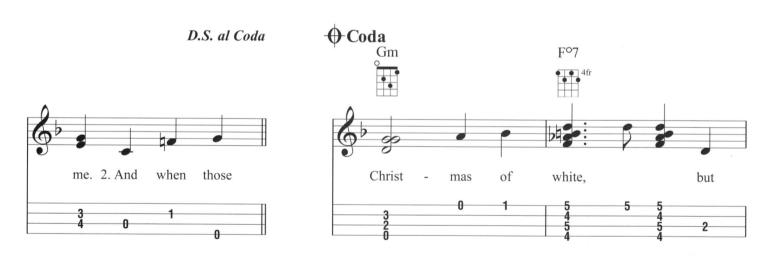

me. 2. And when those

Coda

Christ - mas of white, but

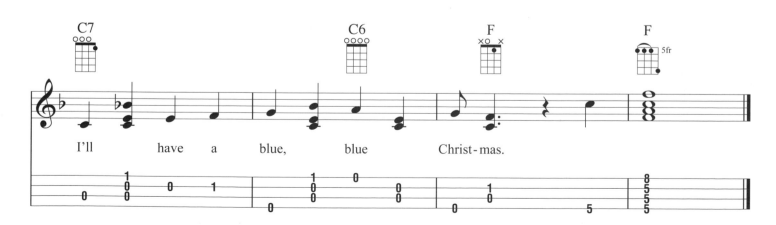

I'll have a blue, blue Christ - mas.

The Christmas Song
(Chestnuts Roasting on an Open Fire)
Music and Lyric by Mel Tormé and Robert Wells

"The Christmas Song" was penned by jazz singer Mel Tormé (known as "the velvet fog," because of his smokey vocals) and his frequent collaborator, Robert Wells, a songwriter/TV producer/script writer. Tormé and Wells were thinking cool thoughts on a hot summer day, and their musings morphed into this tune, which has become one of the most-covered Christmas songs. Nat "King" Cole's 1946 recording, which included a small string section at his behest, first made the ballad famous.

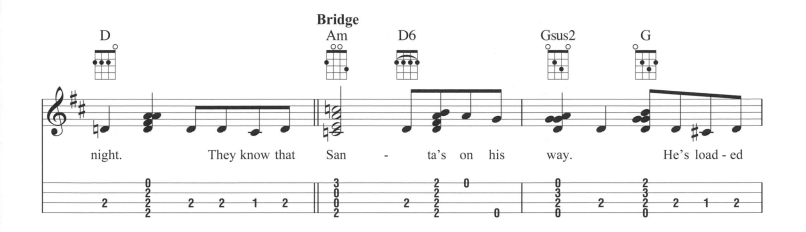

Bridge

night. They know that San - ta's on his way. He's load - ed

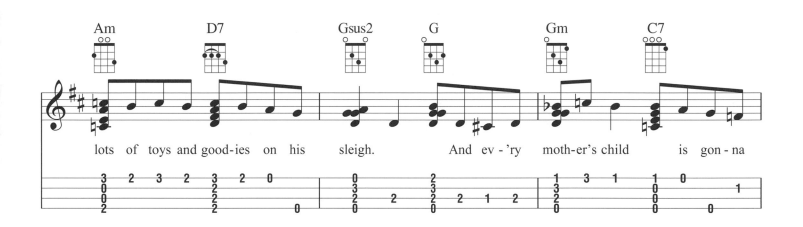

lots of toys and good-ies on his sleigh. And ev-'ry moth-er's child is gon-na

D.C. al Coda

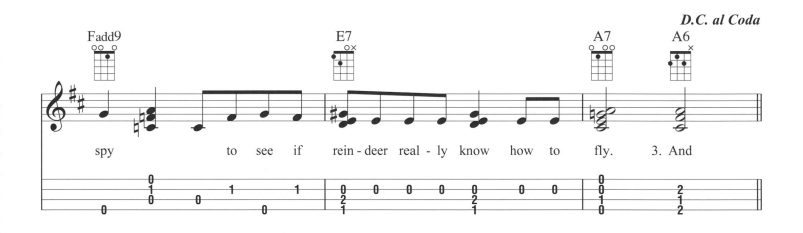

spy to see if rein-deer real-ly know how to fly. 3. And

Coda

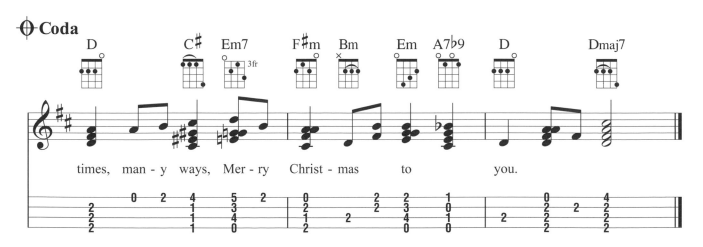

times, man-y ways, Mer-ry Christ-mas to you.

The Christmas Song
(Chestnuts Roasting on an Open Fire)
Music and Lyric by Mel Tormé and Robert Wells

D Em D7 G A7 Bm Gm6 C#7 F#

C7 F F#m B7 Em Am Gsus2 Gm E7

Verse 1
```
        D          Em         D        D7
Chestnuts roasting on an open fire,
        G      A7        Bm   D7
Jack Frost nipping at your nose,
        G      Gm6       D      C#7
Yuletide carols being sung by a choir,
            F#          C7        F
And folks dressed up like Eskimos.
```

Verse 2
```
        A7        D      Em         D        D7
Ev'rybody knows a turkey and some mistletoe
        G      A7        Bm   D7
Help to make the season bright.
        G   Gm6       D      C#7
Tiny tots with their eyes all aglow
            F#m B7      Em   A7 D
Will find it hard to sleep to - night.
```

Bridge
```
                Am  D7          Gsus2
They know that San  -  ta's on his way.
                Am          D7          Gsus2
He's loaded lots of toys and goodies on his sleigh.
              Gm    C7          F
And ev'ry mother's child is gonna spy
              E7                    A7
To see if reindeer really know how to fly.
```

Verse 3
```
        D      Em         D          D7
And so I'm offering this simple phrase
        G      A7        Bm   D7
To kids from one to ninety-two.
        G          Gm6       D      C#7
Although it's been said many times, many ways,
Em    F#m   Bm  Em A7 D
Merry Christ - mas to        you.
```

Christmas Time Is Here

from A CHARLIE BROWN CHRISTMAS
Words by Lee Mendelson
Music by Vince Guaraldi

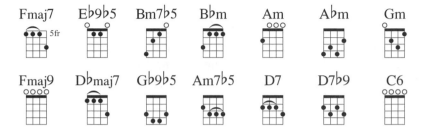

Verse 1

Fmaj7 Eb9b5 Fmaj7 Eb9b5
Christmas time is here, happiness and cheer.

Bm7b5 Bbm Am Abm Gm   Fmaj9
Fun for all that children call their fav'rite time of year.

Verse 2

Fmaj7 Eb9b5 Fmaj7 Eb9b5
Snowflakes in the air, carols everywhere,

Bm7b5 Bbm Am Abm Gm   Fmaj9
Olden times and ancient rhymes of love and dreams to share.

Bridge

Dbmaj7 Gb9b5 Dbmaj7 Gb9b5
Sleigh bells in the air, beauty everywhere.

Am Am7b5 D7 D7b9 Gm Eb9b5 C6
Yuletide by the fireside and joyful mem'ries there.

Verse 3

Fmaj7 Eb9b5 Fmaj7 Eb9b5
Christmas time is here. Families drawing near.

Bm7b5 Bbm Am Abm Gm   Fmaj9
Oh, that we could always see such spirit through the year.

Christmas Time Is Here

from A CHARLIE BROWN CHRISTMAS
Words by Lee Mendelson
Music by Vince Guaraldi

Jazz pianist Vince Guaraldi, who composed and/or recorded several jazz tunes that crossed over and became pop hits, wrote "Christmas Time Is Here" for the 1965 TV animated special *A Charlie Brown Christmas*. He had an assist from TV producer Lee Mendelson, who had been involved in other projects with Charles Schulz, creator of the *Peanuts* comic strip. The award-winning TV show spawned a series of Peanuts programs, its jazz soundtrack became a huge success, and the song became a Christmas standard.

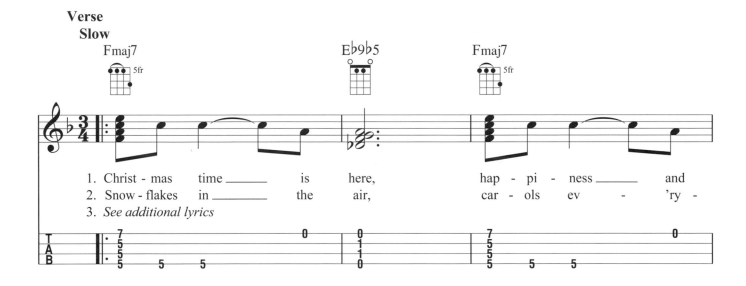

1. Christ - mas time _____ is here, hap - pi - ness _____ and
2. Snow - flakes in _____ the air, car - ols ev - 'ry -
3. *See additional lyrics*

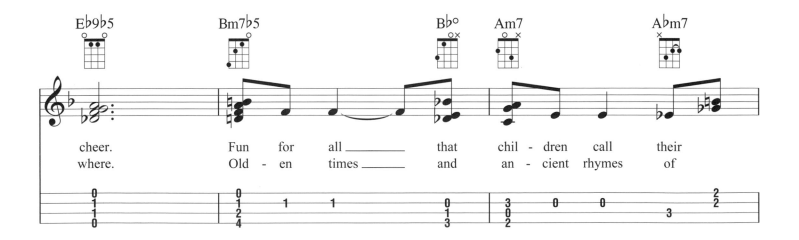

cheer. Fun for all _____ that chil - dren call their
where. Old - en times _____ and an - cient rhymes of

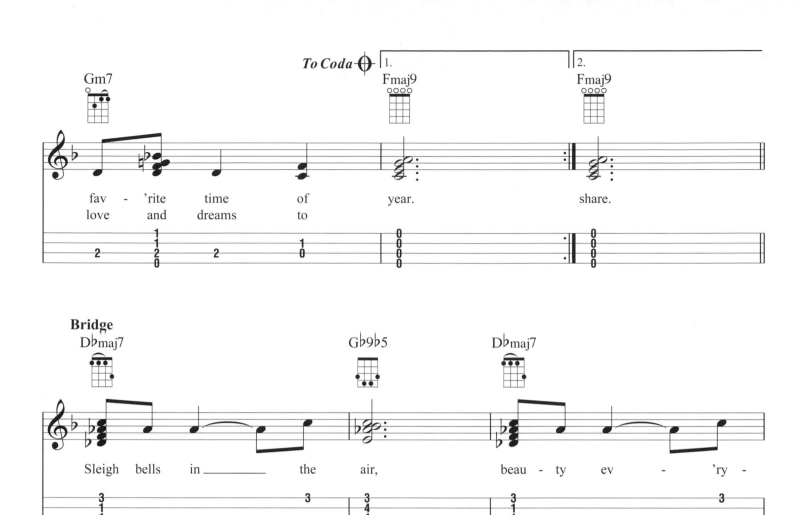

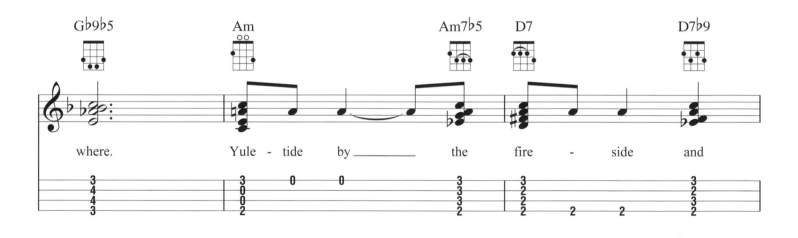

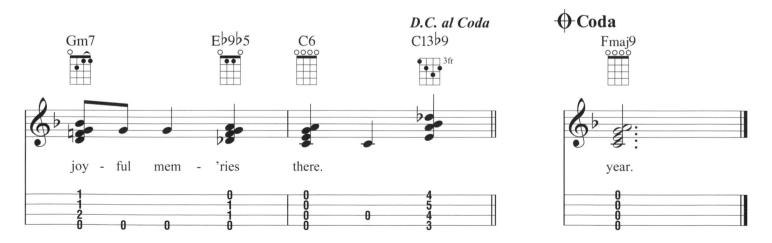

Feliz Navidad

Music and Lyrics by José Feliciano

José Feliciano, the brilliant singer/guitarist, was already internationally famous when he composed and recorded this Christmas song in 1970. He was feeling homesick for his family in Puerto Rico, where people greet each other during the holidays by saying "Feliz Navidad, próspero año y felicidad" (Merry Christmas, a prosperous year and happiness). The tune has grown in popularity over the decades, becoming one of the most-played holiday melodies.

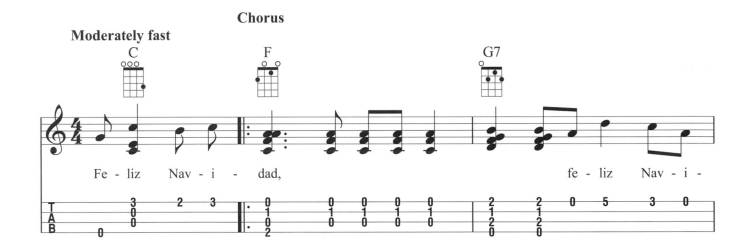

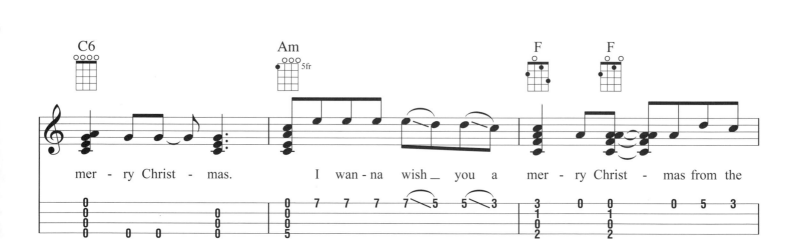

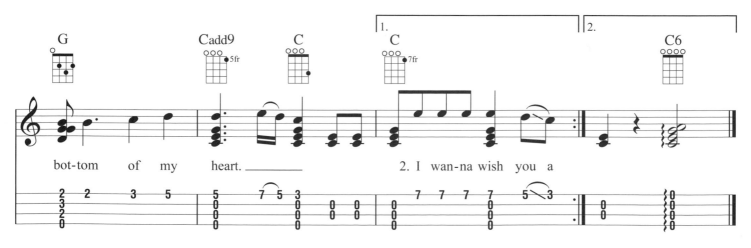

Feliz Navidad

Music and Lyrics by José Feliciano

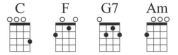

Chorus
```
       C          F   G7       C
Feliz Navidad,    feliz Navidad,
              F           G7        C
Feliz Navidad, próspero año y felicidad.
       C          F   G7       C
Feliz Navidad,    feliz Navidad,
              F           G7        C
Feliz Navidad, próspero año y felicidad.
```

Verse 1
```
       C                    F              G7
I wanna wish you a merry Christmas,
                          C            Am
I wanna wish you a merry Christmas.
                              F
I wanna wish you a merry Christmas from
     G7          C
The bottom of my heart.
```

Verse 2
```
       C                    F              G7
I wanna wish you a merry Christmas,
                          C            Am
I wanna wish you a merry Christmas.
                              F
I wanna wish you a merry Christmas from
     G7          C
The bottom of my heart.
```

Frosty the Snow Man

Words and Music by Steve Nelson and Jack Rollins

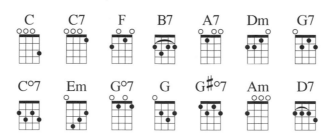

Verse 1

|C |C7 | |F |B7 |C |
Frosty the snow man was a jolly, happy soul,

|F |B7 |C |A7 |Dm |G7 |C |G7 |
With a corncob pipe and a button nose and two eyes made out of coal.

Verse 2

|C |C7 | |F |B7 |C |
Frosty the snow man is a fairy tale, they say.

|F |B7 |C |A7 |Dm |G7 |C |
He was made of snow, but the children know how he came to life one day.

Bridge

|F |C°7 |Em |A7 |Dm |G7 |C |
There must have been some magic in that old silk hat they found,

|G°7 G |G#°7 |Am |D7 |G7 |
For when they placed it on his head, he began to dance around.

Verse 3

|C |C7 | |F |B7 |C |
Frosty the snow man was alive as he could be,

|F |B7 |C |A7 |Dm |G7 |C |
And the children say he could laugh and play just the same as you and me.

Outro

|C | |G7 |
Thumpety thump thump, thumpety thump thump, look at Frosty go,

| |C |
Thumpety thump thump, thumpety thump thump, over the hills of snow.

Additional Lyrics

Verse 4 Frosty the snow man knew the sun was hot that day,
So he said, "Let's run and we'll have some fun now before I melt away."

Verse 5 Down to the village with a broomstick in his hand,
Running here and there, all around the square saying, "Catch me if you can!"

Bridge He led them down the streets of town right to the traffic cop,
And he only paused a moment when he heard him holler, "Stop!"

Verse 6 For Frosty the snow man had to hurry on his way,
But he waved goodbye saying, "Don't you cry, I'll be back again some day."

Outro Thumpety thump thump, thumpety thump thump, look at Frosty go.
Thumpety thump thump, thumpety thump thump, over the hills of snow.

Frosty the Snow Man

Words and Music by Steve Nelson and Jack Rollins

A year after his 1949 hit record "Rudolph the Red-Nosed Reindeer," Gene Autry recorded "Frosty the Snow Man," creating another holiday classic and spawning a cottage industry: A "Little Golden Book" followed, then an animated TV short, and at least four more TV specials thereafter. The song was written by Jack Rollins (who also wrote "Here Comes Peter Cottontail") and Steve Nelson, composer of Tin Pan Alley and country hits.

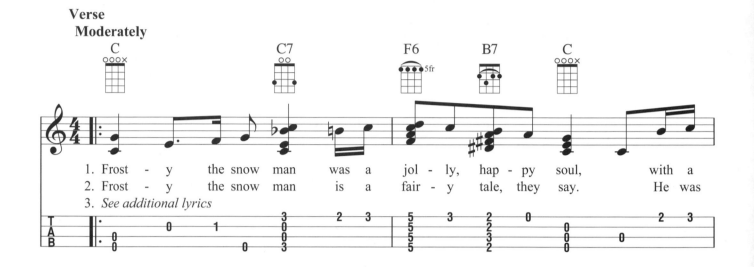

1. Frost - y the snow man was a jol - ly, hap - py soul, with a
2. Frost - y the snow man is a fair - y tale, they say. He was
3. *See additional lyrics*

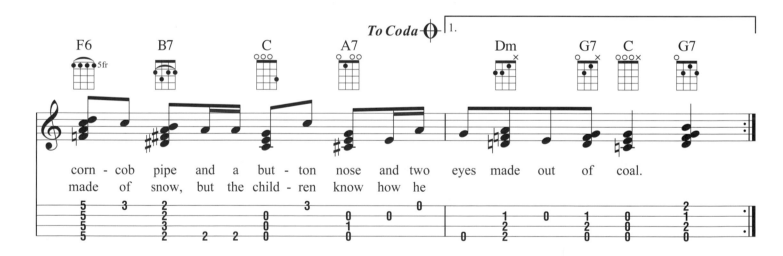

corn - cob pipe and a but - ton nose and two eyes made out of coal.
made of snow, but the child - ren know how he

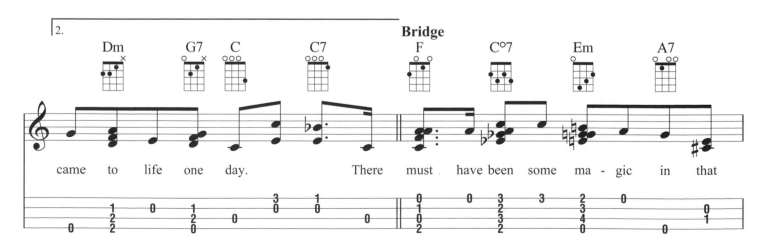

came to life one day. There must have been some ma - gic in that

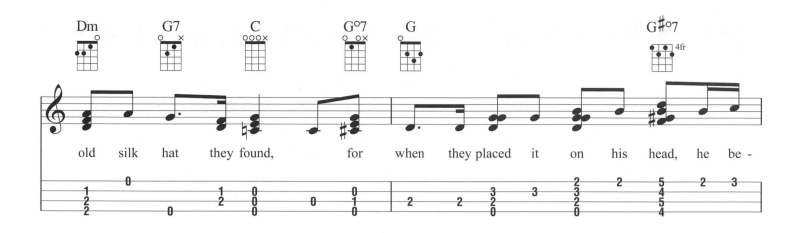

old silk hat they found, for when they placed it on his head, he be-

D.C. al Coda   ⊕ **Coda**

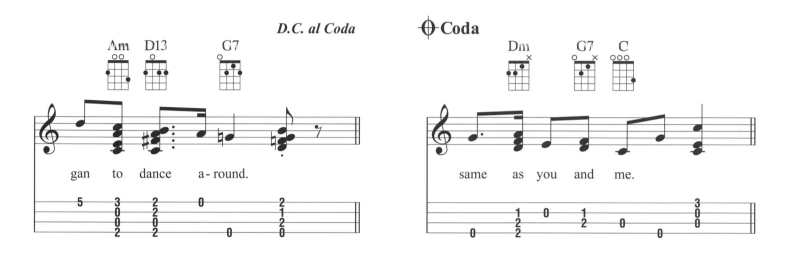

gan to dance a-round.   same as you and me.

Outro

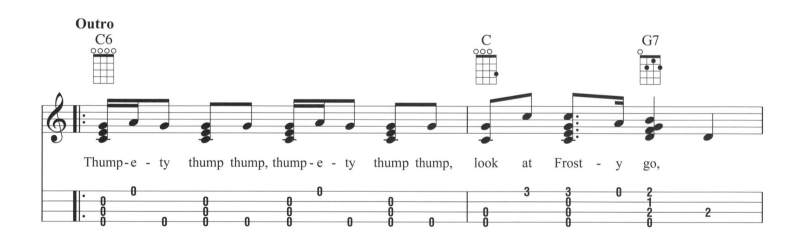

Thump-e-ty thump thump, thump-e-ty thump thump, look at Frost-y go,

thump-e-ty thump thump, thump-e-ty thump thump, o-ver the hills of snow.

Have Yourself a Merry Little Christmas

from MEET ME IN ST. LOUIS
Words and Music by Hugh Martin and Ralph Blane

Judy Garland's poignant rendering of this tune in the 1944 film musical, *Meet Me in St. Louis* made it an instant holiday standard. Hugh Martin and Ralph Blaine wrote all the songs for the movie, including "The Trolley Song" and "The Boy Next Door." When Frank Sinatra recorded the song for a Christmas album, he asked Martin to change the "We'll have to muddle through somehow" line, to make the song more cheerful (the sadder line made sense in the context of the movie)… hence the alternate lyric, "Hang a shining star upon the highest bough."

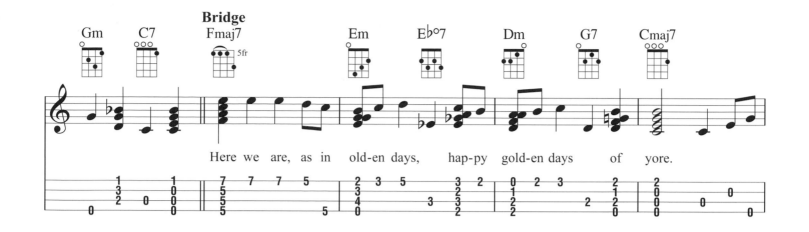

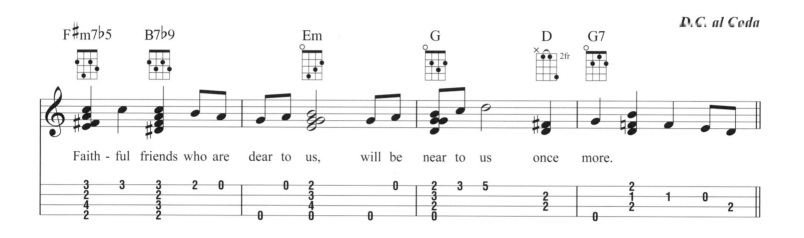

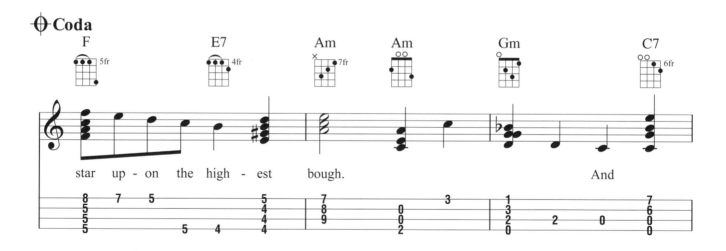

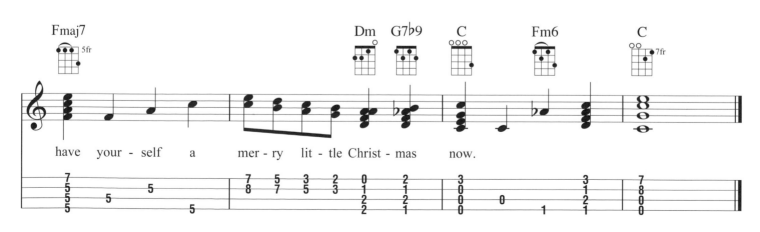

Have Yourself a Merry Little Christmas

from MEET ME IN ST. LOUIS
Words and Music by Hugh Martin and Ralph Blane

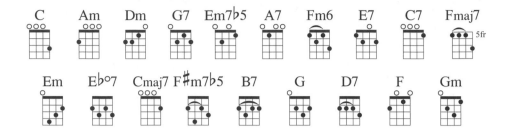

Verse 1
```
        C     Am  Dm       G7
Have yourself a merry little Christmas,

        C     Am  Dm    G7
Let your heart be light.

        C     Am  Dm         G7    Em7b5 A7 Fm6 G7
From now on, our troubles will be out of sight.
```

Verse 2
```
        C     Am  Dm       G7
Have yourself a merry little Christmas,

        C     Am  Dm    G7
Make the Yule tide gay.

        C     Am  Dm       E7    Am   C7
From now on, our troubles will be miles away.
```

Bridge
```
     Fmaj7          Em        Ebo7      Dm       G7  Cmaj7
Here we are as in olden days,      happy golden days   of yore.

     F#m7b5  B7           Em          G     D7    G7
Faithful   friends who are dear to us, gather near to us once more.
```

Verse 3
```
        C      Am   Dm        G7
Through the years we all will be together,

        C     Am  Dm    G7
If the fates allow.

        C      Am   F         E7    Am    Gm   C7
*Hang a shining star upon the highest bough.

        Fmaj7                 Dm    G7  C
And have yourself a merry little Christ - mas now.
```

*Original line: Until then, we'll have to muddle through somehow.

Here Comes Santa Claus
(Right Down Santa Claus Lane)
Words and Music by Gene Autry and Oakley Haldeman

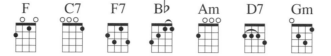

Verse 1

F
Here comes Santa Claus, here comes Santa Claus,
C7
Right down Santa Claus Lane,
                                             F   F7
Vixen and Blitzen and all his reindeer pullin' on the reins.
Bb   C7   Am   D7   Gm C7   F   F7
Bells are ringin', children singin', all is merry and bright.
     Bb   C7   Am   D7
So, hang your stockings and say your prayers
        Gm   C7   F
'Cause Santa Claus comes tonight.

Verse 2

F
Here comes Santa Claus, here comes Santa Claus,
C7
Right down Santa Claus Lane,
                                           F   F7
He's got a bag that's filled with toys for boys and girls again.
Bb   C7   Am D7   Gm   C7   F   F7
Hear those sleigh-bells jingle jangle, oh, what a beautiful sight.
     Bb   C7   Am   D7
So, jump in bed and cover your head
        Gm   C7   F
'Cause Santa Claus comes tonight.

Here Comes Santa Claus

(Right Down Santa Claus Lane)

Words and Music by Gene Autry and Oakley Haldeman

When riding his horse, Champion, in a 1946 Los Angeles Christmas parade, singing cowboy/actor Gene Autry heard the crowd yelling "Here comes Santa Claus!" This inspired him to write the lyrics to his first Christmas song. Autry's 1947 recording of the tune, complete with jingle bell sound effects, was a country and pop hit, and everyone from Bing Crosby to Elvis Presley to Alvin and the Chipmunks has recorded it.

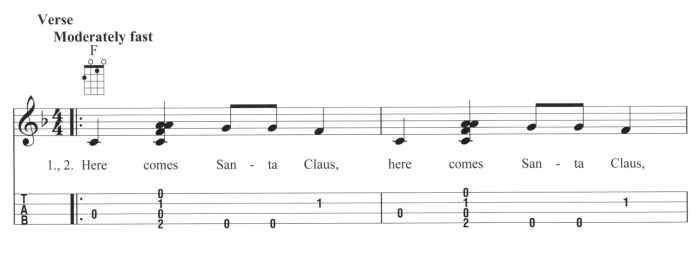

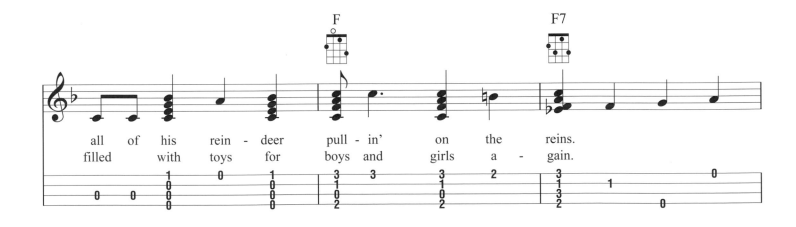

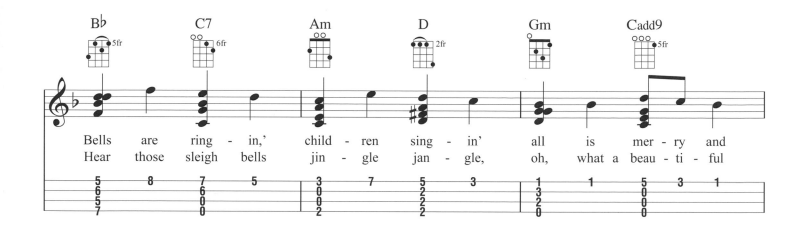

Bells are ring - in,' child - ren sing - in' all is mer - ry and
Hear those sleigh bells jin - gle jan - gle, oh, what a beau - ti - ful

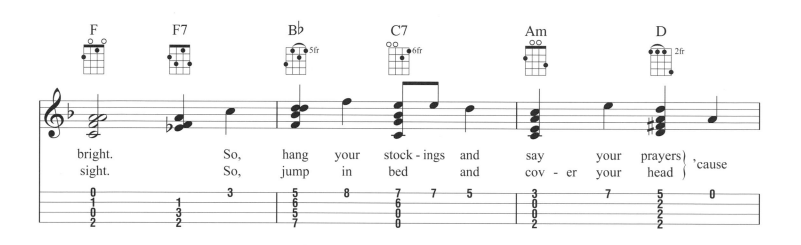

bright. So, hang your stock - ings and say your prayers) 'cause
sight. So, jump in bed and cov - er your head }

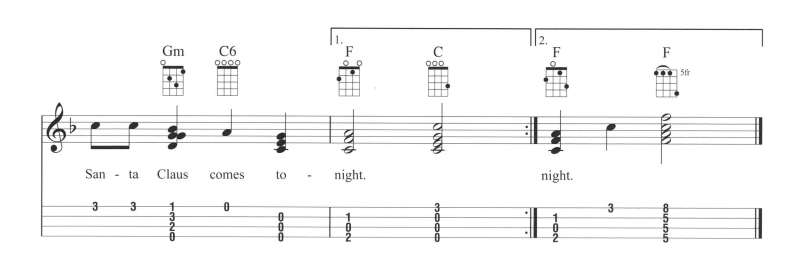

San - ta Claus comes to - night.   night.

I'll Be Home for Christmas

Words and Music by Kim Gannon and Walter Kent

"I'll Be Home for Christmas" was written by Walter Kent (["There'll be Bluebirds Over] The White Cliffs of Dover") and Kim Gannon ("Moonlight Cocktail," "A Dreamer's Holiday") in 1943. That same year, Bing Crosby's hit recording of the tune brought a tear to the eye of many an American soldier overseas in World War II.

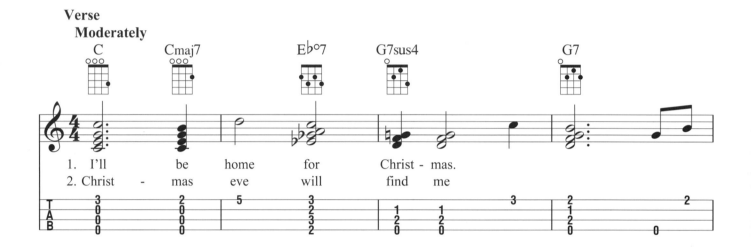

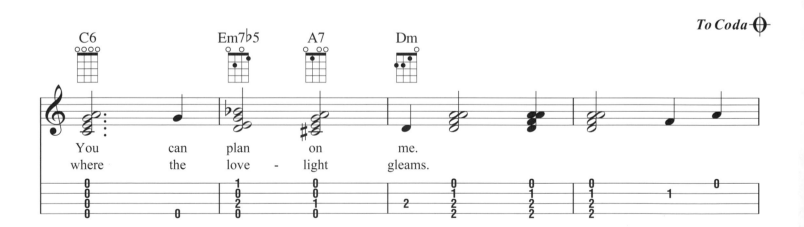

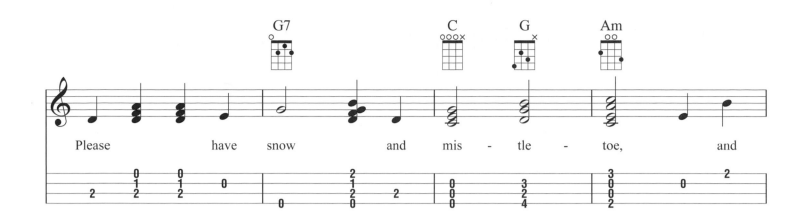

Please have snow and mis - tle - toe, and

D.C. al Coda

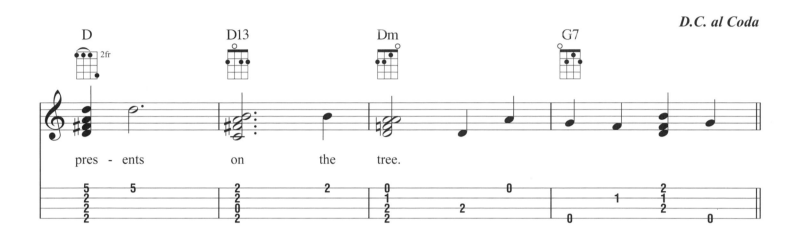

pres - ents on the tree.

Ø Coda

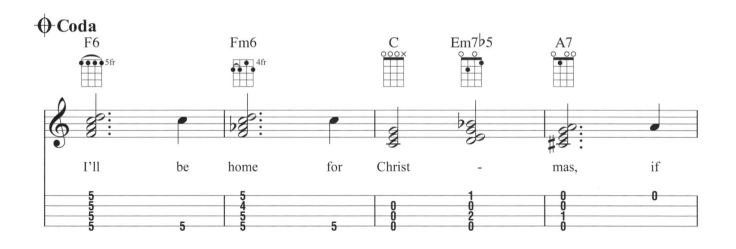

I'll be home for Christ - mas, if

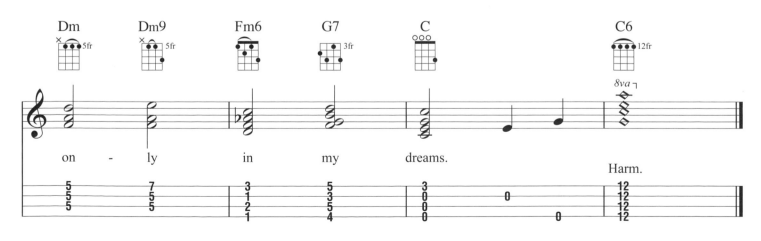

on - ly in my dreams.

Harm.

I'll Be Home for Christmas

Words and Music by Kim Gannon and Walter Kent

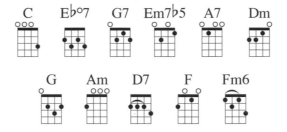

Verse 1

C   E♭°7   G7
I'll be home for Christmas.
C   Em7♭5 A7 Dm
You can plan   on me.
           G7   C   G   Am
Please have snow and mis - tle - toe,
     D7   Dm G7
And presents on the tree.

Verse 2

C   E♭°7   G7
Christmas Eve will find me
C   Em7♭5 A7 Dm
Where the love - light gleams.
F   Fm6   C Em7♭5 A7
I'll be home for Christ - mas,
 Dm Fm6 G7 C
If only in   my dreams.

Let It Snow! Let It Snow! Let It Snow!

Words by Sammy Cahn
Music by Jule Styne

             F   C7   F
Verse 1 Oh, the weather outside is frightful,

                   G7 C7
But the fire is so delightful,

       Gm   D7   G7   C7   F
And since we've no place to go, let it snow, let it snow, let it snow.

             F   C7   F
Verse 2 It doesn't show signs of stopping,

                       G7   C7
And I brought some corn for popping.

       Gm   D7   G7   C7   F
The lights are turned way down low. Let it snow, let it snow, let it snow.

             C   Dm   G7   C
Bridge When we finally kiss good-night, how I'll hate going out in the storm.

                                D7   G7   C7
But if you really hold me tight, all the way home I'll be warm.

             F   C7   F
Verse 3 The fire is slowly dying,

                     G7   C7
And, my dear, we're still good - bye - ing,

       Gm   D7   G7   C7   F
But as long as you love me so, let it snow, let it snow, let it snow.

Let It Snow! Let It Snow! Let It Snow!

Words by Sammy Cahn
Music by Jule Styne

Like "The Christmas Song," "Let It Snow" was written in 1945 on a hot summer day in Los Angeles. That year, it was a No. 1 hit for vocalist Vaughn Monroe, and it has joined the list of essential holiday tunes, though it never mentions Christmas. The composer and lyricist are both responsible for multiple hits in The Great American Songbook: Jule Styne composed "Just in Time," "I Don't Want to Walk Without You," "Time After Time," "People," and "Make Someone Happy," just to name a few. Sammy Cahn wrote lyrics for "Three Coins in a Fountain," "The Tender Trap," "I'll Walk Alone," "Come Fly with Me," "The Christmas Waltz," and many more classics.

1. Oh, the weath-er out-side is fright-ful, but the fire is so de-light-ful, and since we've no place to go, let it snow, let it snow, let it snow. 2. It

does-n't show signs of stop-ping, and I brought some corn for pop-ping. The lights are turned way down low,

3. *See additional lyrics*

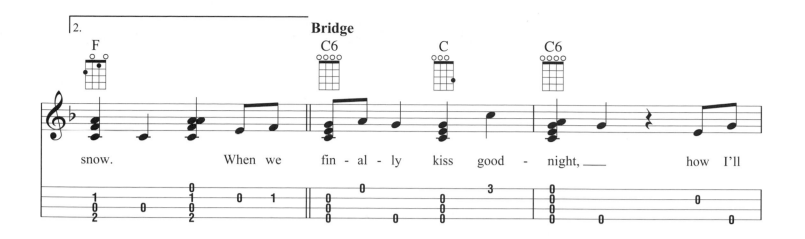

snow.   When we   fin - al - ly   kiss   good - night, ____   how I'll

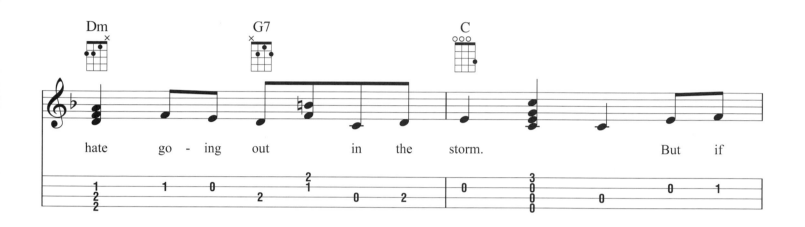

hate   go - ing   out   in   the   storm.   But   if

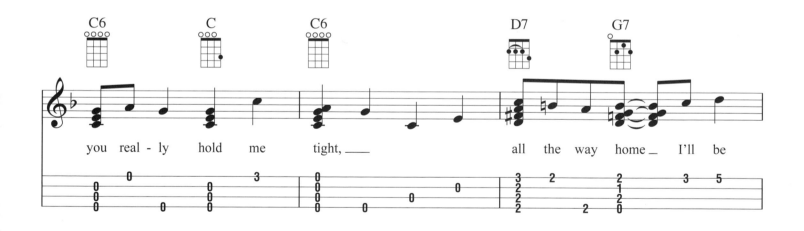

you   real - ly   hold   me   tight, ____   all   the   way   home __   I'll   be

D.S. al Coda   **Coda**

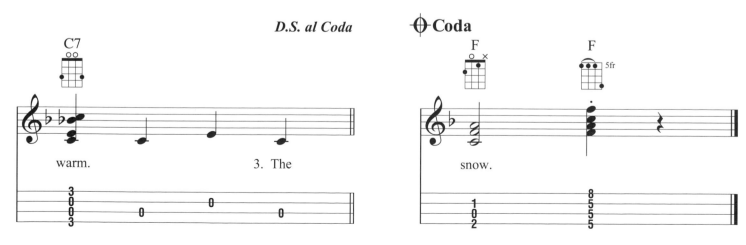

warm.   3. The   snow.

It's Beginning to Look Like Christmas

By Meredith Willson

Meredith Willson, famous for writing *The Music Man* and other Broadway musicals, wrote the words and music to "It's Beginning to Look Like Christmas" in 1951. It was a hit for Perry Como and for Bing Crosby that same year, and has become a holiday standard. In the lyrics – "Hopalong," a TV cowboy, Hopalong Cassidy, and "the five-and-ten," a type of low-priced variety store – reference the early '50s era.

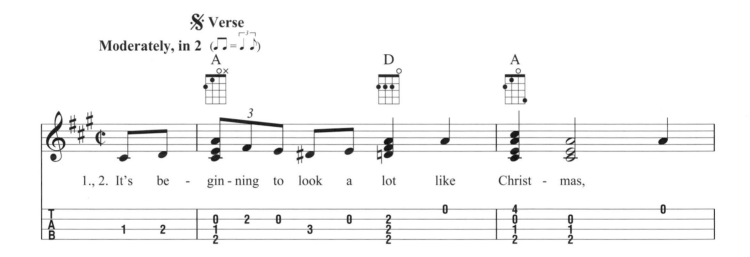

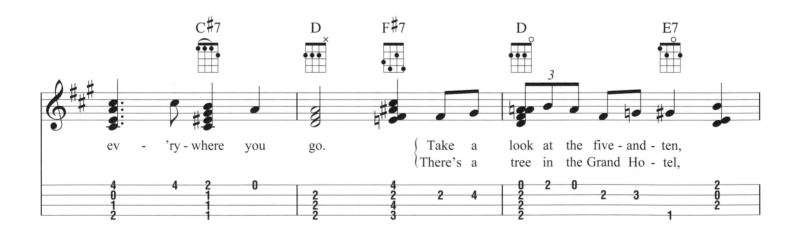

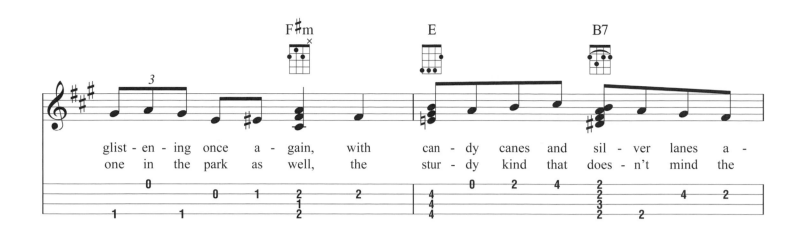

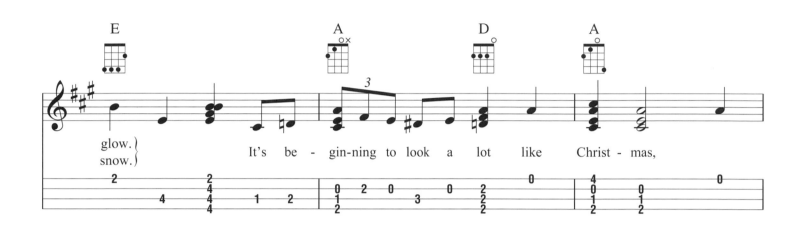

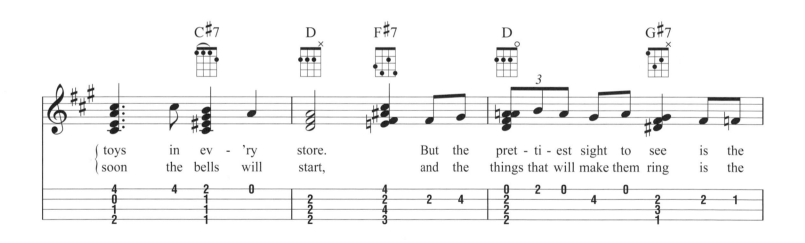

To Coda ⊕

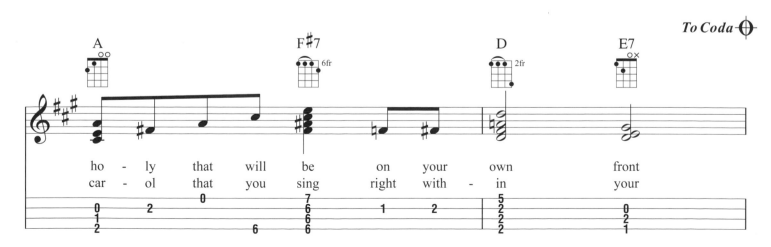

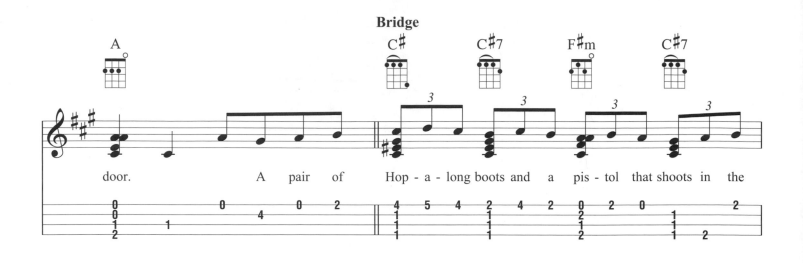

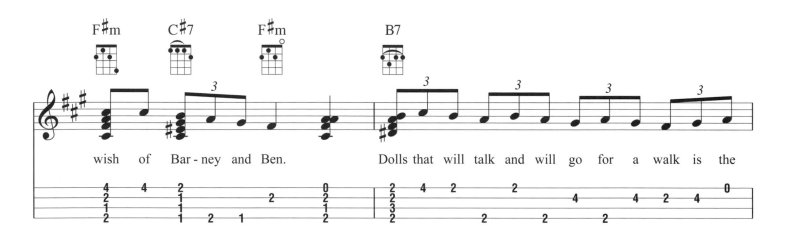

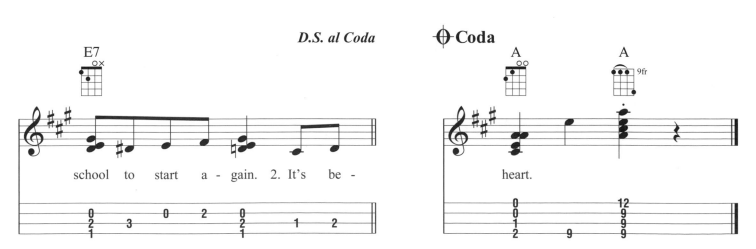

It's Beginning to Look Like Christmas

By Meredith Willson

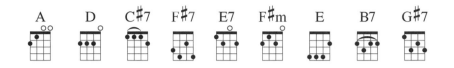

Verse 1
```
        A                D      A          C#7      D    F#7
It's beginning to look a lot like Christmas, ev'rywhere you go.
        D              E7            F#m
Take a look in the five-and-ten, glistening once again,
        E            B7          E7
With candy canes and silver lanes aglow.
        A                D      A          C#7  D
It's beginning to look a lot like Christmas, toys in ev'ry store,
                          G#7    A          F#7
But the prettiest sight to see is the holly that will be
        D  E7  A
On your own front door.
```

Bridge
```
        C#7                F#m      C#7
A pair of Hopalong boots and a pistol that shoots
        F#m   C#7      F#m
Is the wish of Barney and Ben.
B7
Dolls that will talk and will go for a walk
        E       B7       E
Is the hope of Janice and Jen.
        E7
And Mom and Dad can hardly wait for school to start again.
```

Verse 2
```
        A                D      A          C#7      D    F#7
It's beginning to look a lot like Christmas, ev'rywhere you go.
        D              E7                  F#m
There's a tree in the Grand Hotel, one in the park as well,
        E            B7            E7
The sturdy kind that doesn't mind the snow.
        A                D      A          C#7      D
It's beginning to look a lot like Christmas, soon the bells will start,
                          G#7    A          F#7
And the thing that will make them ring is the carol that you sing
        D  E7  A
Right within your heart.
```

Jingle Bell Rock

Words and Music by Joe Beal and Jim Boothe

Country singer Bobby Helms first recorded "Jingle Bell Rock" in 1957, when rock 'n' roll, as a musical genre, was only a few years old. That same year, Helms also had hits with "Fraulein" and "My Special Angel." Two businessmen, Joe Beal and Jim Boothe, are credited as writers of "Jingle Bell Rock." However, Hank Garland, whose brilliant guitar licks are heard throughout Helms's recording, always claimed that he and Bobby Helms completely changed Beal and Boothe's song around until it was a totally different tune and lyric – and that's the version that has become a Christmas standard.

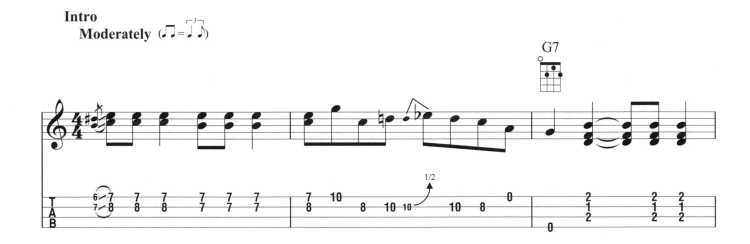

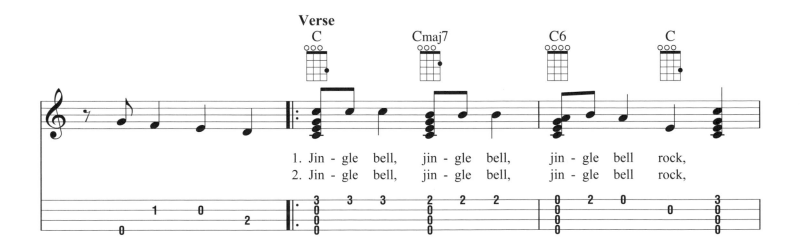

1. Jin - gle bell, jin - gle bell, jin - gle bell rock,
2. Jin - gle bell, jin - gle bell, jin - gle bell rock,

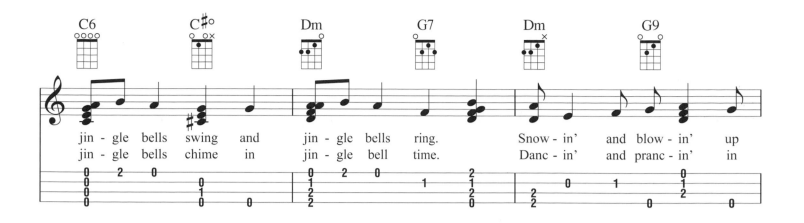

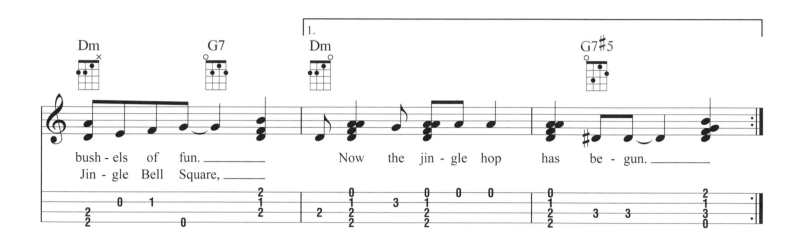

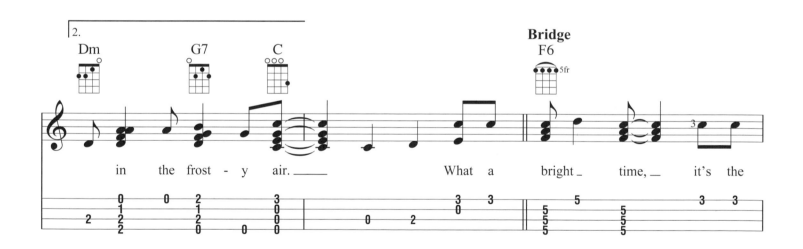

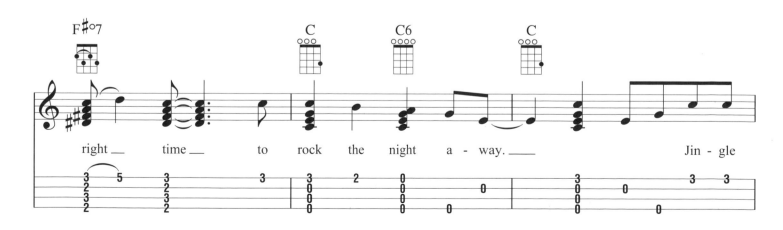

bell ___ time ___ is a swell ___ time ___ to go glid-in' in a

Outro

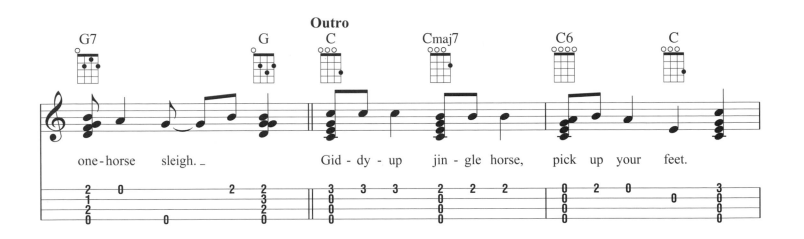

one-horse sleigh. _ Gid-dy-up jin-gle horse, pick up your feet.

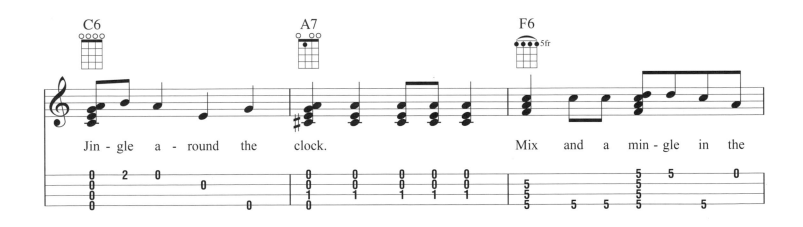

Jin-gle a-round the clock. Mix and a min-gle in the

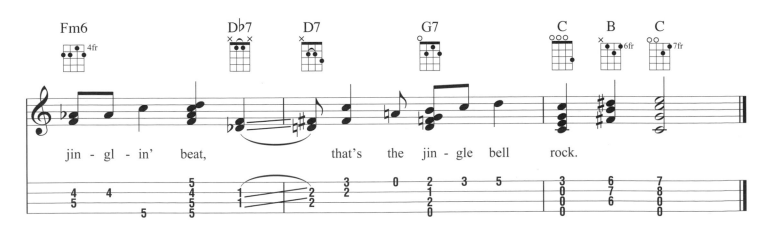

jin-gl-in' beat, that's the jin-gle bell rock.

Jingle Bell Rock

Words and Music by Joe Beal and Jim Boothe

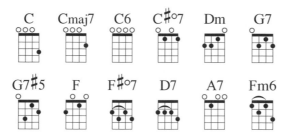

Verse 1
  C   Cmaj7 C6   C
Jingle bell, jingle bell, jingle bell rock,
      C#°7 Dm   G7
Jingle bells swing and jingle bells ring.
Dm   G7   Dm   G7
Snowin' and blowin' up bushels of fun.
Dm   G7#5
Now the jingle hop has begun.

Verse 2
  C   Cmaj7 C6   C
Jingle bell, jingle bell, jingle bell rock,
      C#°7 Dm   G7
Jingle bells chime in jingle bell time.
Dm   G7   Dm   G7 Dm   G7 C
Dancin' and prancin' in Jingle Bell Square, in the frosty air.

Bridge
       F   F#°7   C
What a bright time, it's the right time to rock the night away.
      D7   G7
Jingle bell time is a swell time to go glidin' in a one-horse sleigh.

Outro
  C   Cmaj7 C6   C   A7
Giddy-up jingle horse, pick up your feet. Jingle around the clock.
F   Fm6
Mix and a mingle in the jinglin' beat,
D7   G7   C
That's the jingle bell rock.

Mele Kalikimaka

Words and Music by R. Alex Anderson

R. Alex Anderson was born in Hawaii and composed nearly 200 *hapa haole** songs (based on Hawaiian themes, they combine English and Hawaiian lyrics), including the famous "Lovely Hula Hands." He wrote "Mele Kalikimaka" in 1949 and played and sang it for his friend Bing Crosby, who surprised Anderson by recording it. There are no *r* or *s* sounds in the Hawaiian language, so mele kalikimaka is a Hawaiian approximation of "merry Christmas." (*Hapa haole's true definition is half Hawaiian and half white.)

Mele Kalikimaka

Words and Music by R. Alex Anderson

G   G°7   D7   Am   Dm   G7   C   E7   A7

Verse 1

G   G°7   D7
Mele Kalikimaka is the thing to say on a bright Hawaiian Christmas day.
                                    Am
That's the island greeting that we send to you,
                    D7   G
From the land where palm trees sway.
Dm   G7   C
Here we know that Christmas will be green and bright.
    E7   A7   D7
The sun will shine by day and all the stars at night.
G   E7   Am   D7   G   Am   D7
Mele Kalikimaka is Hawaii's way to say a Merry Christmas to you.

Verse 2

G   G°7   D7
Mele Kalikimaka is the thing to say on a bright Hawaiian Christmas day.
                                    Am
That's the island greeting that we send to you,
                        D7   G
From the land where the coconut trees sway.
Dm   G7   C
Here we know that Christmas will be green and bright.
    E7   A7   D7
The sun will shine by day and all the stars at night.
G   E7   Am   D7   G
Mele Kalikimaka is Hawaii's way to say a Merry Christmas to you.

The Most Wonderful Time of the Year

Words and Music by Eddie Pola and George Wyle

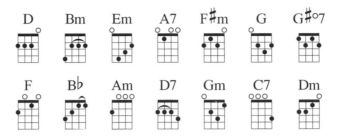

Verse 1
```
        D  Bm     Em A7    D  Bm Em A7
It's the most wonderful time    of the year,
        Em      A7      F#m    Bm       G                G#°7
With the kids jingle belling and ev'ryone telling you, "Be of good cheer."
        F#m Bm     Em A7      D  F  Bb A7
It's the most wonderful time    of the year.
```

Verse 2
```
        D  Bm     Em A7      D  Bm Em A7
It's the hap - happiest sea - son of all,
        Em       A7      F#m       Bm       G                G#°7
With those holiday greetings and gay happy meetings when friends come to call.
        F#m Bm     Em A7      Am   D7
It's the hap - happiest sea - son of all.
```

Bridge
```
        G       G#°7        F#m       Bm
There'll be parties for hosting, marshmallows for toasting
    Em      A7        D
And caroling out in the snow.
        Gm       C7       F       Dm    Em                    A7
There'll be scary ghost stories and tales of the glories of Christmases long, long ago.
```

Verse 3
```
        D  Bm     Em A7      D  Bm Em A7
It's the most wonderful time    of the year.
        Em      A7      F#m       Bm       G                G#°7
There be much mistletoeing and hearts will be glowing when loved ones are near.
        F#m Bm     Em A7      D  Bb  D
It's the most wonderful time    of the year.
```

The Most Wonderful Time of the Year

Words and Music by Eddie Pola and George Wyle

Popular vocalist Andy Williams had a weekly TV show throughout the 1960s; his vocal music director, George Wyle, co-wrote "The Most Wonderful Time of the Year" with Edward Pola for a 1963 Christmas special. Williams sang it every year when the season came around. Like other songs in this collection, it became an international holiday standard, performed and recorded by countless singers.

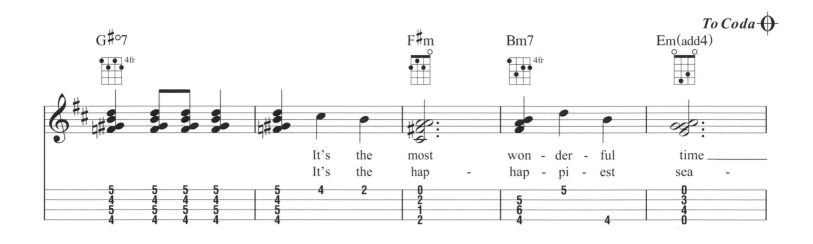

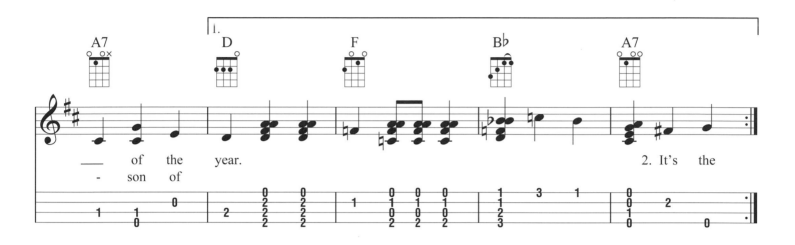

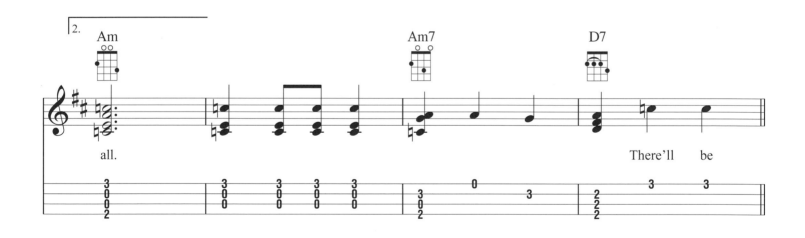

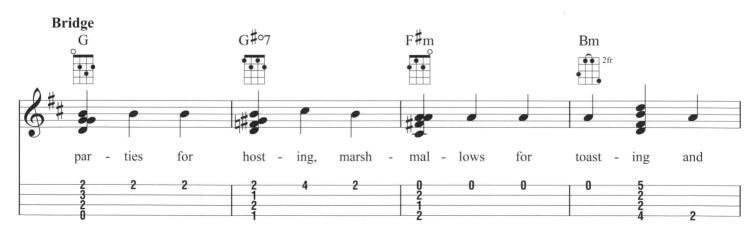

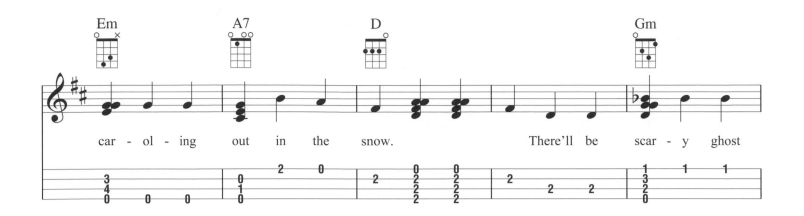

car - ol - ing out in the snow. There'll be scar - y ghost

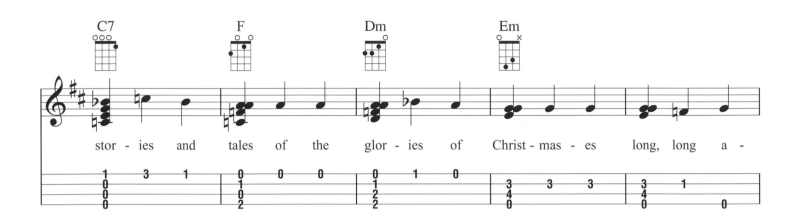

stor - ies and tales of the glor - ies of Christ - mas - es long, long a -

D.S. al Coda Coda

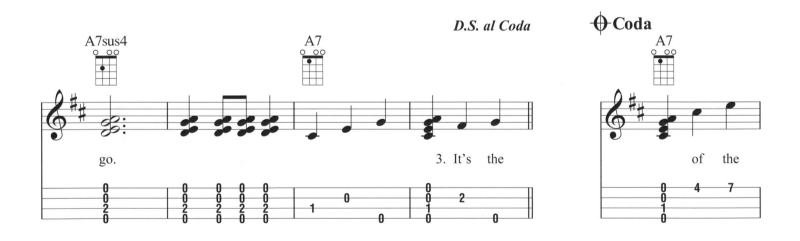

go.   3. It's the   of the

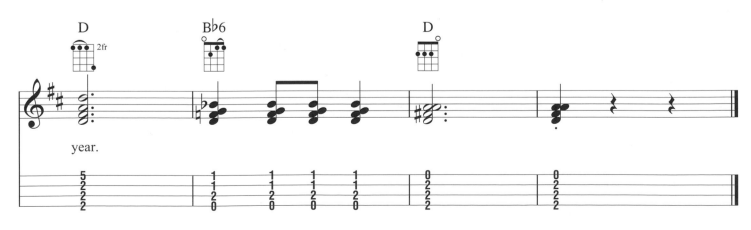

year.

Rockin' Around the Christmas Tree

Music and Lyrics by Johnny Marks

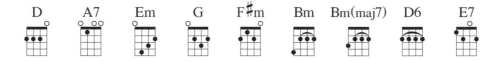

Verse 1
D
Rockin' around the Christmas tree
A7
At the Christmas party hop,
Em   A7   Em   A7   D
Mistletoe hung where you can see ev-'ry couple tries to stop,

Verse 2
D
Rockin' around the Christmas tree,
A7
Let the Christmas spirit ring,
Em   A7   Em   A7   D
Later we'll have some pumpkin pie, and we'll do some caroling.

Bridge
G   F♯m
You will get a sentimental feeling when you hear,
Bm   Bm(maj7) D6
Voices singing,   "Let's be jolly,
E7   A7
Deck the halls with boughs of holly."

Verse 3
D
Rockin' around the Christmas tree,
A7
Have a happy holiday,
Em   A7   Em   A7
Ev-'ryone dancin' merri - ly
                              D
In the new old-fashioned way.

Rockin' Around the Christmas Tree

Music and Lyrics by Johnny Marks

Brenda Lee was only 13 years old in 1958, when she recorded "Rockin' Around the Christmas Tree." It eventually became her biggest-selling record (over 25 million copies), in a career that included 47 charting hits during the 1960s. Johnny Marks, who also wrote "A Holly Jolly Christmas" and another song about a certain reindeer, wrote "Rockin' Around…" in response to the rock 'n' roll craze that was only a few years old. He asked Brenda Lee to sing it, even though she had not enjoyed major success with previous record releases. His hunch was correct: her voice, along with an ace Nashville studio band that included Hank Garland on guitar, sold the song. And it keeps on selling.

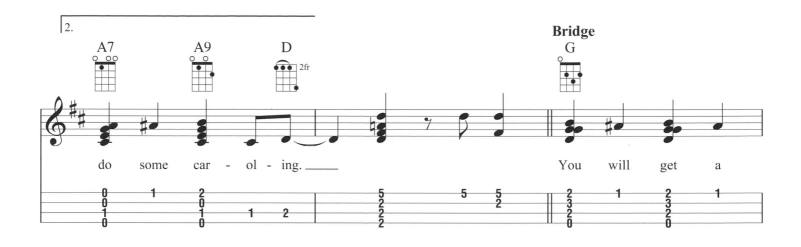

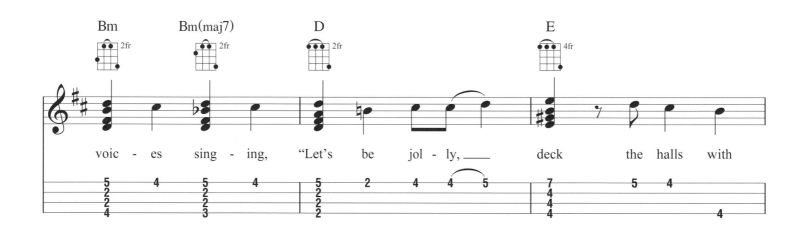

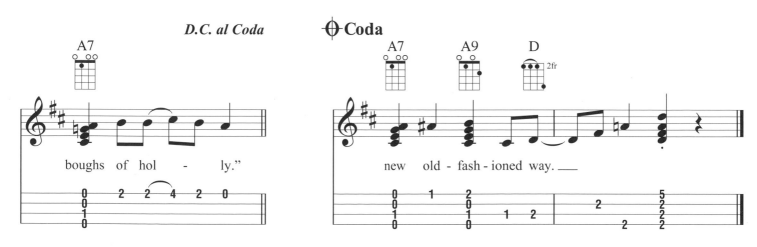

My Favorite Things

from THE SOUND OF MUSIC

Lyrics by Oscar Hammerstein II
Music by Richard Rodgers

"My Favorite Things" was written by Rodgers and Hammerstein and sung first by Mary Martin in the 1959 Broadway show *The Sound of Music*. However, more people have heard Julie Andrews sing it in the 1965 movie version. It has become a jazz standard, thanks to John Coltrane's 1960, 14-minute instrumental recording. Though it never mentions Christmas, the song is included regularly in holiday programs, albums, music books, and performances.

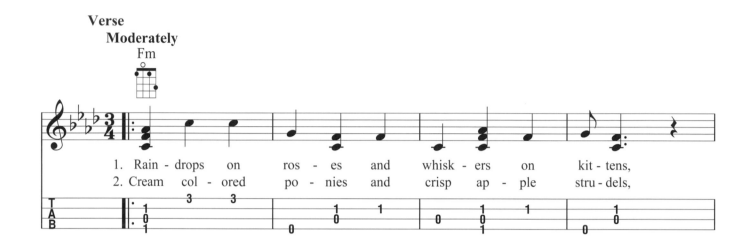

1. Rain - drops on ros - es and whisk - ers on kit - tens,
2. Cream col - ored po - nies and crisp ap - ple stru - dels,

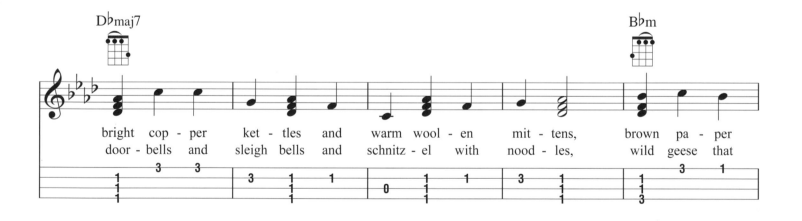

bright cop - per ket - tles and warm wool - en mit - tens, brown pa - per
door - bells and sleigh bells and schnitz - el with nood - les, wild geese that

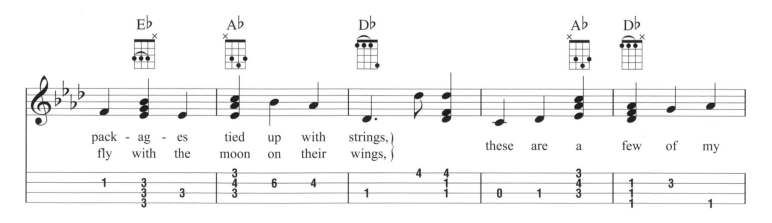

pack - ag - es tied up with strings, }
fly with the moon on their wings, } these are a few of my

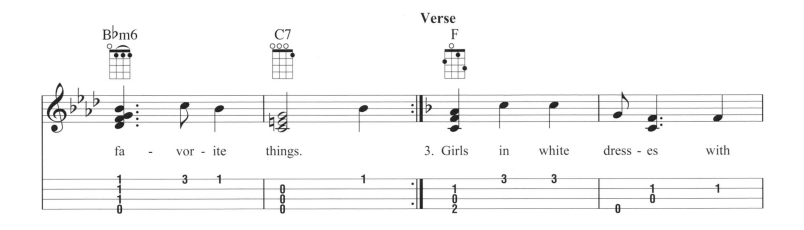

fa - vor - ite things. 3. Girls in white dress - es with

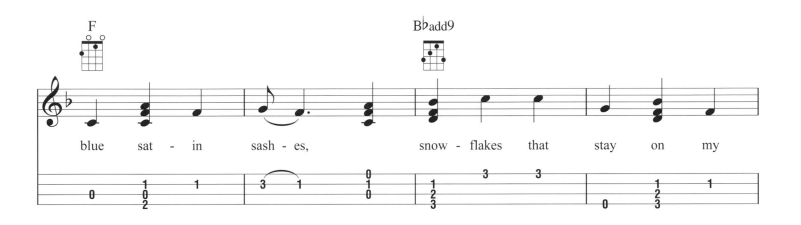

blue sat - in sash - es, snow - flakes that stay on my

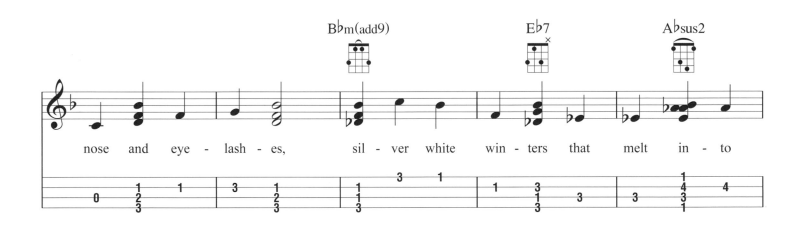

nose and eye - lash - es, sil - ver white win - ters that melt in - to

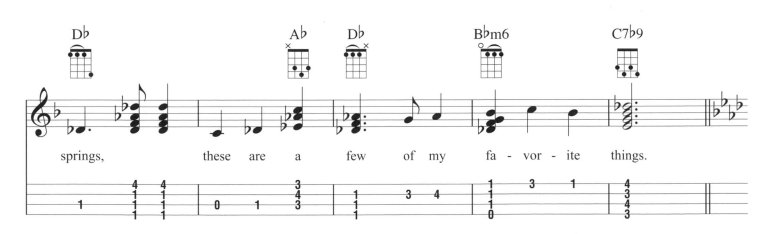

springs, these are a few of my fa - vor - ite things.

Outro

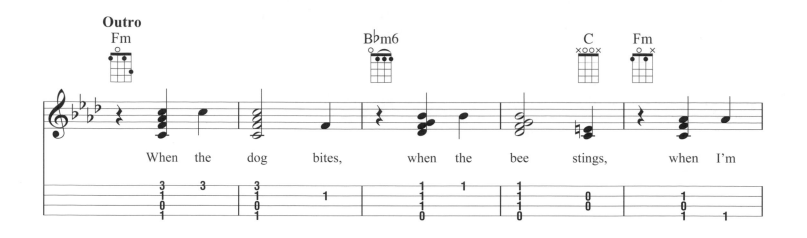

When the dog bites, when the bee stings, when I'm

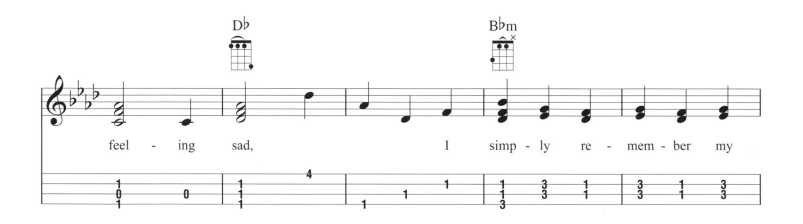

feel - ing sad, I simp - ly re - mem - ber my

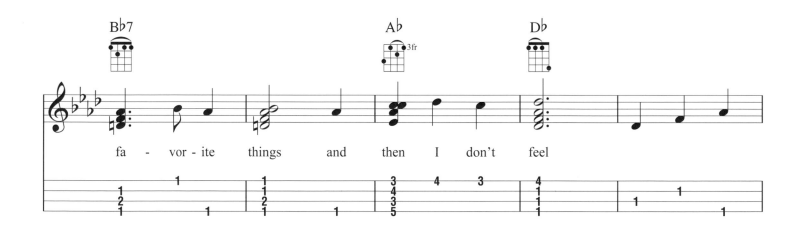

fa - vor - ite things and then I don't feel

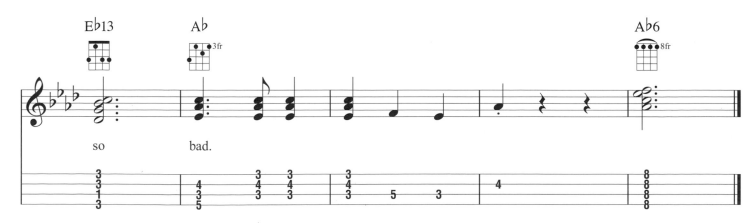

so bad.

My Favorite Things

from THE SOUND OF MUSIC
Lyrics by Oscar Hammerstein II
Music by Richard Rodgers

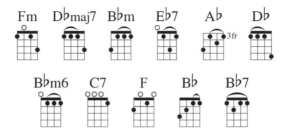

Verse 1
Fm
Raindrops on roses and whiskers on kittens,
D♭maj7
Bright copper kettles and warm woolen mittens,
B♭m   E♭7   A♭   D♭
Brown paper packages tied up with strings,
A♭   D♭   B♭m6   C7
These are a few of my favorite things.

Verse 2
Fm
Cream-colored ponies and crisp apple strudels,
D♭maj7
Doorbells and sleigh bells and schnitzel with noodles,
B♭m   E♭7   A♭   D♭
Wild geese that fly with the moon on their wings,
A♭   D♭   B♭m6   C7
These are a few of my favorite things.

Verse 3
F
Girls in white dresses with blue satin sashes,
B♭
Snowflakes that stay on my nose and eyelashes,
B♭m   E♭7   A♭   D♭
Silver white winters that melt into springs,
A♭   D♭   B♭m6   C7
These are a few of my favorite things.

Outro
Fm   B♭m6   C7   Fm   D♭
When the dog bites,   when the bee stings,   when I'm feeling sad,
    B♭m   B♭7   A♭   D♭ E♭7 A♭
I simply remember my favorite things and then I don't feel   so   bad.

Rudolph the Red-Nosed Reindeer

Music and Lyrics by Johnny Marks

In 1939, an advertising copywriter named Robert L. May created the Rudolph character for Montgomery Ward Department Stores, who published a Christmas pamphlet telling the story of the reindeer with a shiny nose. In 1947, the store gave May the copyright of his verse, and a book was published with some success. Two years later, May's songwriting brother-in-law, Johnny Marks, set the verse to music and asked Gene Autry to record it. Autry didn't like the song, but his wife convinced him to record it, pointing out that Rudolph was an underdog, and Americans love an underdog! She was right: It became Autry's and Marks's biggest hit, with cover versions whose record sales topped 150 million, second only to "White Christmas." Later, Marks wrote "A Holly Jolly Christmas," "Rockin' Around the Christmas Tree" and (for Chuck Berry) "Run Rudolph Run."

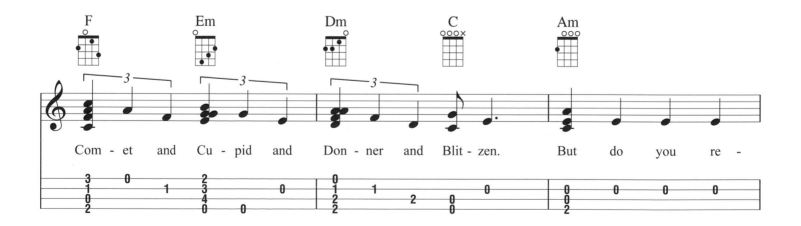

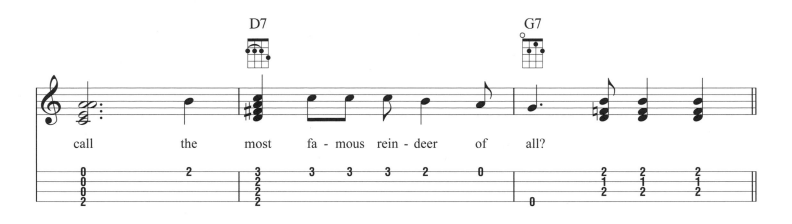

call the most fa - mous rein - deer of all?

𝄋 Verse
a tempo

1. Ru - dolph, the red - nosed rein - deer   had a ver - y shin - y
2. All of the oth - er rein - deer   used to laugh and call him
3. Then how the rein - deer loved him,   as they shout - ed out with

To Coda ⊕

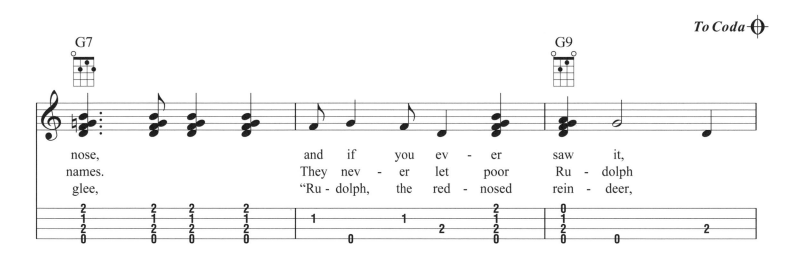

nose,   and if you ev - er saw it,
names.   They nev - er let poor Ru - dolph
glee,   "Ru - dolph, the red - nosed rein - deer,

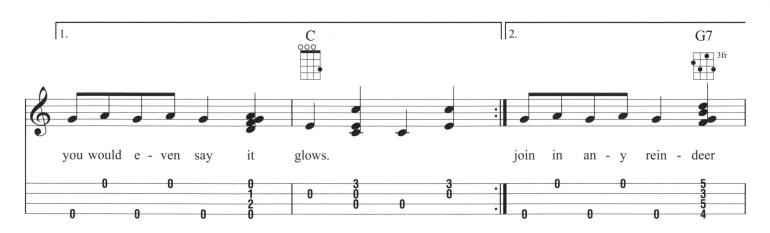

1.
you would e - ven say it glows.

2.
join in an - y rein - deer

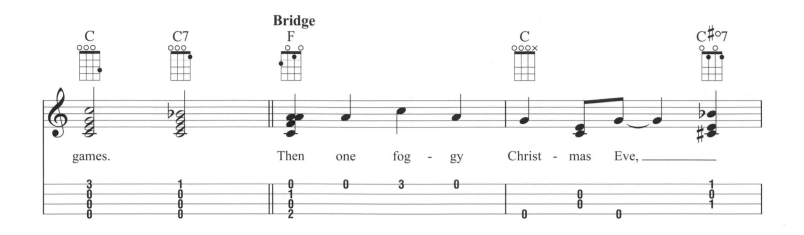

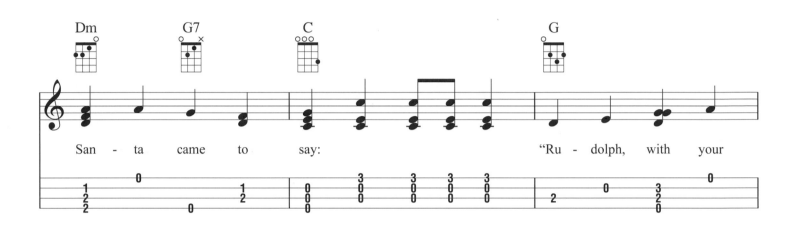

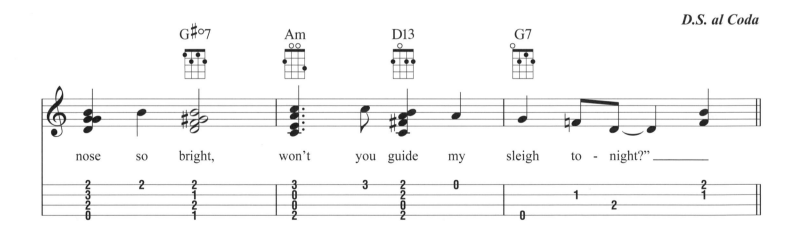

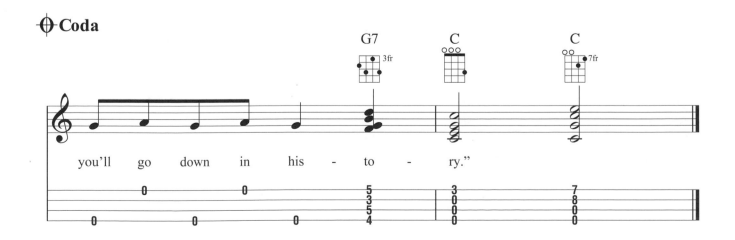

Rudolph the Red-Nosed Reindeer

Music and Lyrics by Johnny Marks

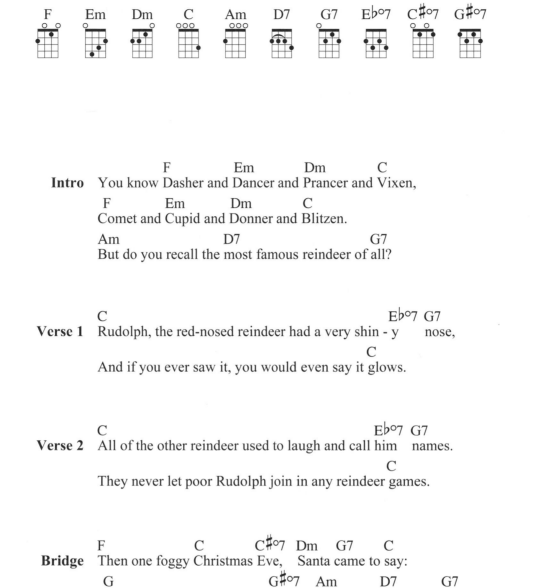

	F Em Dm C
Intro	You know Dasher and Dancer and Prancer and Vixen,

         F   Em   Dm   C
Comet and Cupid and Donner and Blitzen.

Am   D7   G7
But do you recall the most famous reindeer of all?

       C   E♭°7 G7
Verse 1 Rudolph, the red-nosed reindeer had a very shin - y   nose,

                             C
And if you ever saw it, you would even say it glows.

       C   E♭°7 G7
Verse 2 All of the other reindeer used to laugh and call him   names.

                             C
They never let poor Rudolph join in any reindeer games.

       F   C   C♯°7 Dm G7   C
Bridge Then one foggy Christmas Eve,   Santa came to say:

   G   G♯°7 Am   D7   G7
"Rudolph, with your nose so bright, won't you guide my sleigh tonight?"

       C   E♭°7 G7
Verse 3 Then how the reindeer loved him, as they shouted out with glee,

                             C
"Rudolph, the red-nosed reindeer, you'll go down in history!"

Santa Baby

By Joan Javits, Phil Springer and Tony Springer

"Santa Baby" was co-written in 1953 by Joan Javits and prolific songwriter Philip Springer, who claims to have written the music in ten minutes. They were commissioned to create a Christmas song for Eartha Kitt, whose performance of the tune was so suggestive that it was banned by radio stations in the Southern U.S. The controversy only helped sales, and "Santa Baby" became the biggest-selling Christmas song of 1953 – and went on to become a staple holiday hit, covered by divas such as Madonna, Kylie Minogue, Taylor Swift. Ariana Grande, Trisha Yearwood, and Gwen Stefani.

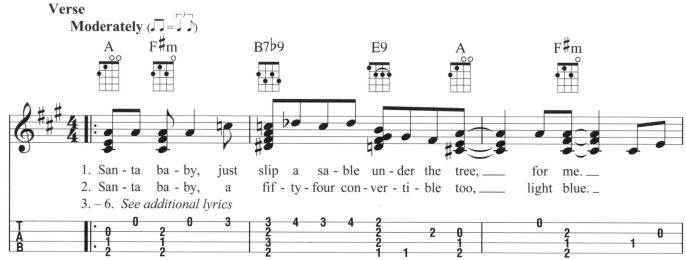

1. San-ta ba-by, just slip a sa-ble un-der the tree, ___ for me.
2. San-ta ba-by, a fif-ty-four con-ver-ti-ble too, ___ light blue. _
3. – 6. *See additional lyrics*

Note: Play song twice through to include all additional lyrics.

Been an aw-ful good girl, ___
I'll wait up for you, dear, ___

San-ta ba-by, so

hur-ry down the chim-ney to-night. ___

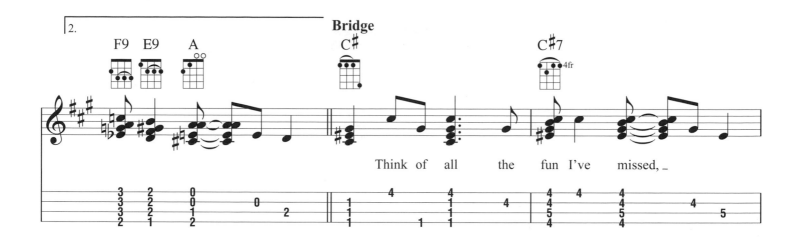

Think of all the fun I've missed, __

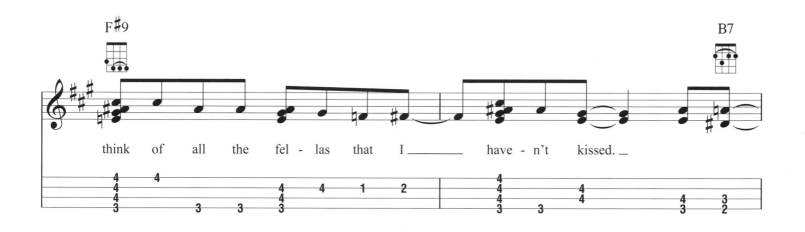

think of all the fel - las that I _____ have - n't kissed. __

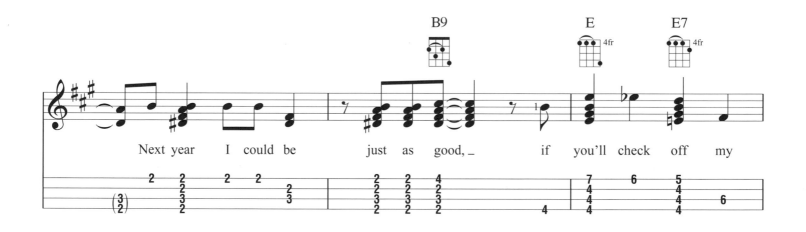

Next year I could be just as good, __ if you'll check off my

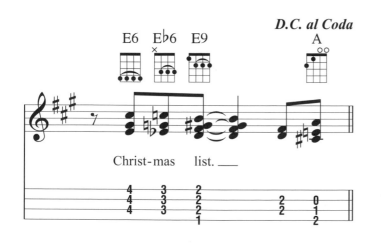

Christ - mas list. __

Santa Baby

By Joan Javits, Phil Springer and Tony Springer

A   F#m   B7   E7   Bm   F7   C#7   F#7   D

Verse 1

A   F#m   B7   E7   A   F#m B7   E7   A
Santa baby, just slip a sable under the tree, for me.   Been an awful good girl,
     F#m   B7   E7   A   F#m   Bm E7 A
Santa baby, so hurry down the chimney tonight.

Verse 2

A   F#m   B7   E7   A   F#m B7   E7   A
Santa baby, a '54 convertible too, light blue.   I'll wait up for you, dear,
       F#m   Bm   E7   A   F#m   F7 E7 A
Santa baby, so hurry down the chimney tonight.

Bridge 1

C#7   F#7
Think of all the fun I've missed, think of all the fellas that I haven't kissed.
B7   E7
Next year I could be just as good, if you'll check off my Christmas list.

Verse 3

A   F#m   B7   E7   A   F#m B7   E7   A
Santa baby, I wanna yacht, and really that's not a lot.   Been an angel all year,
       F#m   Bm   E7   A   F#m   Bm E7 A
Santa baby, so hurry down the chimney tonight.

Verse 4

A   F#m   B7   E7   A   F#m B7   E7   A
Santa honey, there's one little thing I really do need: the deed   to a platinum mine,
       F#m   Bm   E7   A   F#m   Bm E7 A
Santa honey, so hurry down the chimney tonight.

Verse 5

A   F#m   B7   E7   A   F#m B7   E7   A
Santa cutie, and fill my stocking with a duplex, and checks.   Sign your 'X' on the line,
       F#m   Bm   E7   A   F#m   F7 E7 A
Santa cutie, and hurry down the chimney tonight.

Bridge 2

C#7   F#7
Come and trim my Christmas tree with some decorations bought at Tiffany's,
B7   E7
I really do believe in you, let's see if you believe in me.

Verse 6

A   F#m   B7   E7   A   F#m B7   E7   A
Santa baby, forgot to mention one little thing, a ring.   I don't mean on the phone,
       F#m   Bm   E7   A   D A
Santa baby, so hurry down the chimney tonight.

Santa Claus Is Comin' to Town

Words by Haven Gillespie
Music by J. Fred Coots

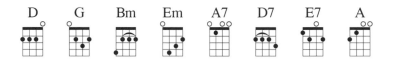

D   G   Bm   Em   A7   D7   E7   A

Verse 1
       D   G
You better watch out, you better not cry,
   D   G
Better not pout, I'm telling you why:
   D   Bm   Em   A7 D   A7
Santa Claus is coming to   town.

Verse 2
        D   G
He's making a list, he's checking it twice.
        D   G
He's gonna find out who's naughty or nice.
   D   Bm   Em   A7   D
Santa Claus is coming to   town.

Bridge
       D7   G   D7   G
He sees you when you're sleeping. He knows when you're awake.
   E7   A   E7   A7
He knows if you've been bad or good, so be good for goodness sake.

Verse 3
       D   G
You better watch out, you better not cry,
   D   G
Better not pout, I'm telling you why:
   D   Bm   Em   A7 D
Santa Claus is coming to   town.

Santa Claus Is Comin' to Town

Words by Haven Gillespie
Music by J. Fred Coots

A 1934 recording by banjoist Harry Reser introduced this song to the public, and the same year Eddie Cantor sang it on his radio show. It was a hit in 1934 and was eventually covered by over 200 artists, including Bing Crosby, Frank Sinatra, Bruce Springsteen, The Temptations, and the Jackson 5. The composers were J. Fred Coots ("You Go to My Head," "For All We Know," and many more standards) and Haven Gillespie ("That Lucky Old Sun," "Breezin' Along with the Breeze," "Right or Wrong," among others).

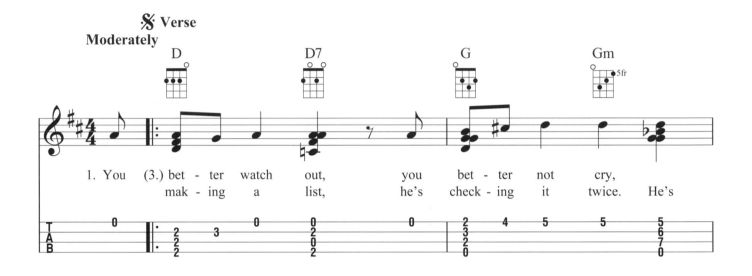

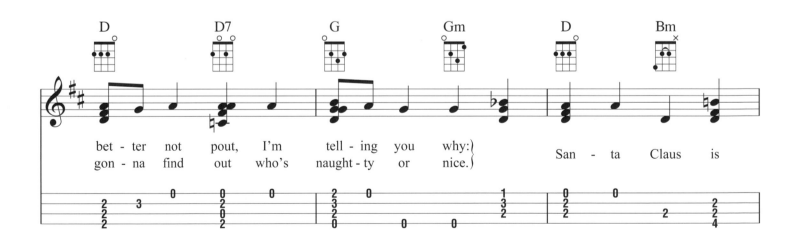

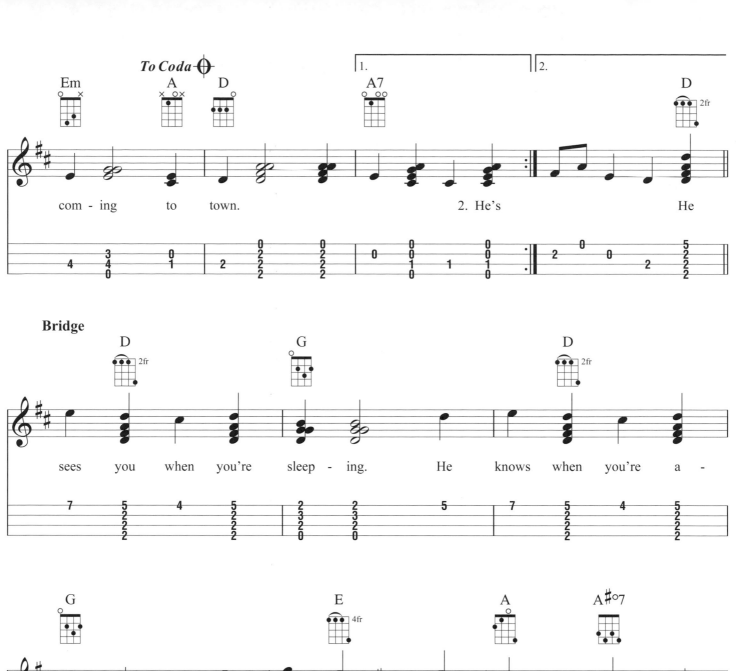

To Coda ⊕

Em   A   D   A7 | 1. | 2.   D

com- ing   to town.   2. He's   He

Bridge

D   G   D

sees   you   when   you're   sleep - ing.   He   knows   when   you're   a -

G   E   A   A♯°7

wake.   He   knows   if   you've   been   bad   or   good,   so   be

D.S. al Coda   ⊕ **Coda**

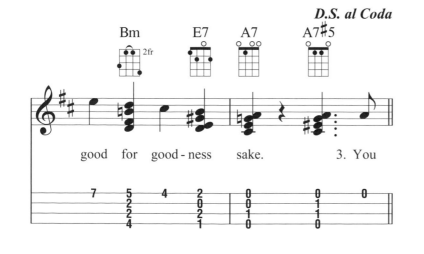

Bm   E7   A7   A7♯5

good   for   good- ness   sake.   3. You

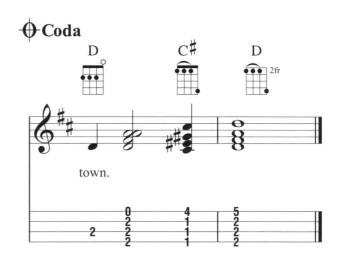

D   C♯   D

town.

Silver Bells

from the Paramount Picture THE LEMON DROP KID
Words and Music by Jay Livingston and Ray Evans

The highly successful songwriting team of Jay Livingston and Ray Evans penned "Silver Bells" in 1934. Their list of compositions includes the movie songs "Buttons and Bows," "Mona Lisa," and "Que Sera, Sera," all of which won Academy Awards. They originally wrote "Tinkle Bells," until Livingston's wife pointed out the public's unfortunate association with the word "tinkle." The song was popularized in 1950, when Bob Hope and Marilyn Maxwell sang it in the film *The Lemon Drop Kid*, and that same year, Bing Crosby's recording pushed the song to greater success. Today, it turns up on nearly every Christmas album.

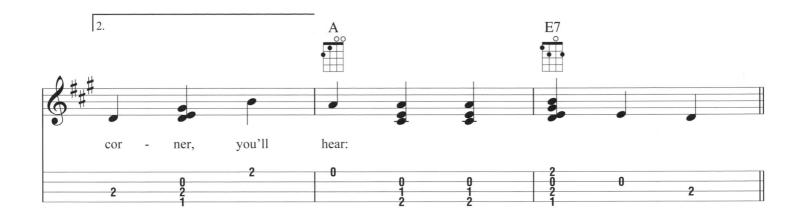

cor - ner, you'll hear:

Chorus

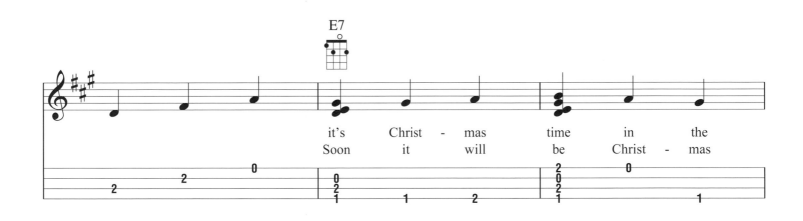

Sil - ver bells, sil - ver bells,
Ring - a - ling, hear them ring.

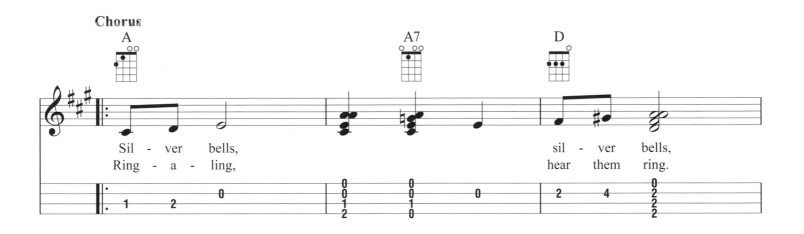

it's Christ - mas time in the
Soon it will be Christ - mas

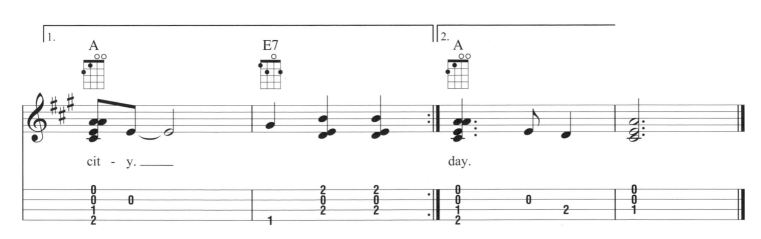

cit - y. _____ day.

Silver Bells

from the Paramount Picture THE LEMON DROP KID

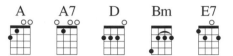

          A   A7   D   Bm

Verse 1 City sidewalks, busy sidewalks, dressed in holiday style,

          E7   A   E7

In the air there's a feeling of Christmas.

          A   A7   D   Bm

Verse 2 Children laughing, people passing, meeting smile after smile,

          E7   A   E7

And on ev'ry street corner you'll hear:

          A   A7 D   E7   A   E7

Chorus Silver bells,   silver bells, it's Christmas time in the city.

          A   A7 D   E7   A

Ring-a-ling,   hear them ring. Soon it will be Christmas day.

What Are You Doing New Year's Eve?

By Frank Loesser

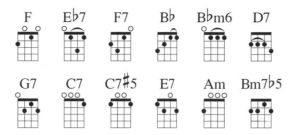

Verse 1

F　　　　　　　　Eb7
Maybe it's much too early in the game,
F　　　F7　　　Bb　　　　　Bbm6
Ah, but I thought I'd ask you just the same.
F　　　　　D7　　G7　　　　C7　C7♯5　F　　C7
What are you doing New Year's, New Year's Eve?

Verse 2

F　　　　　　　　Eb7
Wonder whose arms will hold you good and tight
F　　　F7　Bb　　　　　　Bbm6
When it's exactly twelve o'clock that night,
F　　　　　D7　　G7　　　C7　　　　　F　　　E7
Welcoming in the new year, New Year's Eve.

Bridge

Am　　　　　　Bm7b5　　E7　Am　　　　　　　　Bm7b5　E7
Maybe I'm crazy to sup - pose 　　 I'd ever be the one you chose
Am　　　　　　　D7　　　　　G7　　　C7
Out of a thousand 　　 invitations you'll receive.

Verse 3

F　　　　　　　　Eb7
Ah, but in case I stand one little chance,
F　　　　F7　　　Bb　　　　　　Bbm6
Here comes the jackpot question in advance:
F　　　　　D7　　G7　　　C7　　　　　F
What are you doing New Year's, New Year's Eve?

What Are You Doing New Year's Eve?

By Frank Loesser

Frank Loesser wrote "What Are You Doing New Year's Eve?" in 1947. The Orioles took the song to the Top 10 of 1947's R&B charts. It has since become a holiday standard. Loesser was a prolific composer who often wrote both words and music for Broadway musicals and stand-alone pop songs. His hits include the musicals *Guys and Dolls* and *How to Succeed in Business Without Really Trying,* and the songs "Baby, It's Cold Outside" (an Academy Award winner), "Two Sleepy People," "On a Slow Boat to China," "I Don't Want to Walk Without You," "Heart and Soul," and too many more to mention.

1. May-be it's much too ear-ly in the game,
2. Won-der whose arms will hold you good and tight
3. *See additional lyrics*

ah, but I thought I'd ask you just the same. What are you do-ing
when it's ex-act - ly twelve o'-clock that night, wel-com-ing in the

New Years's, New Year's Eve?
new year,

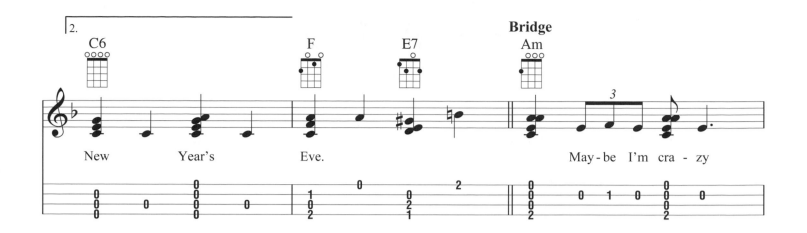

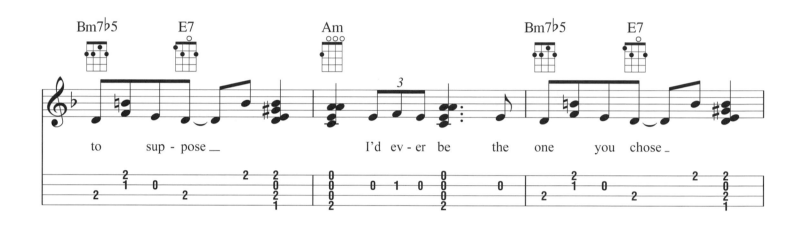

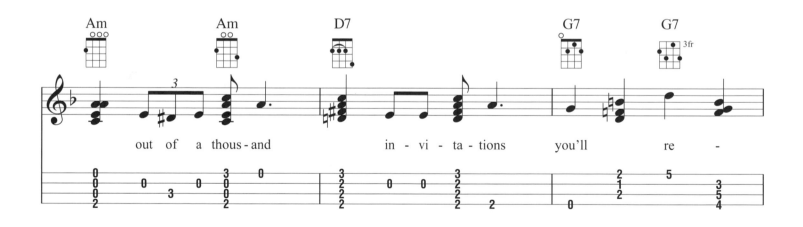

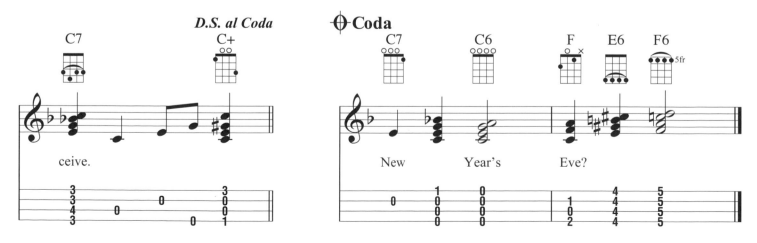

Sleigh Ride

Music by Leroy Anderson
Words by Mitchell Parish

Leroy Anderson, composer of light concert music, wrote "Sleigh Ride" in 1948, as an orchestral instrumental piece. A few years later, Mitchell Parish wrote the lyrics that are heard today. Parish also penned lyrics for "Stardust," "Sophisticated Lady," "Sweet Lorraine," "Deep Purple," and many more standards of The Great American Songbook. The most musically complex of the holiday song genre, "Sleigh Ride" has three sections and numerous key changes.

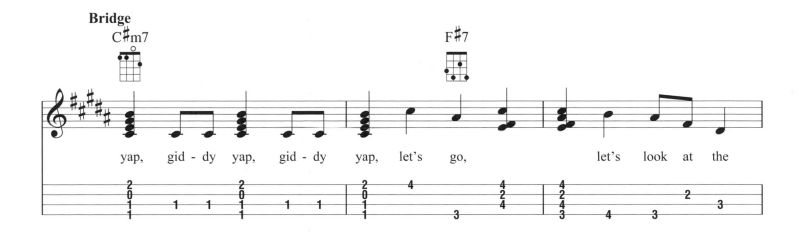

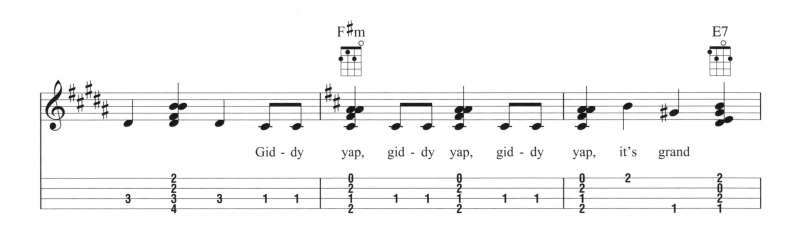

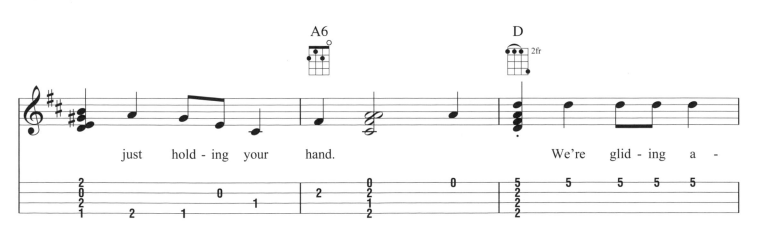

long with a song of a win-ter-y fair-y - land. 2. Our cheeks are

⊕ Coda 1   **Bridge**

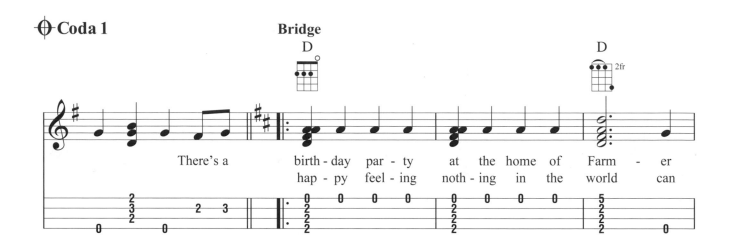

There's a   birth-day par-ty   at   the home of Farm - er
hap-py feel-ing   noth-ing in   the   world can

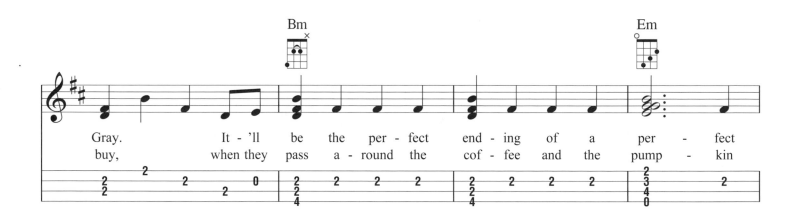

Gray.   It - 'll be   the per - fect   end - ing of   a   per - fect
buy,   when they pass a - round the   cof - fee and the   pump - kin

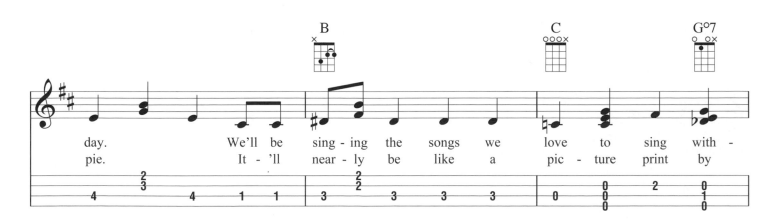

day.   We'll be   sing - ing the songs we   love to sing with -
pie.   It - 'll near - ly be like a   pic - ture print by

out   a   sin - gle   stop,   at   the   fire - place   while   we
Cur - ri - er   and

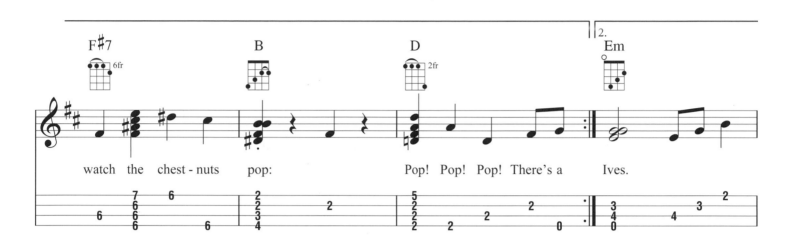

watch   the   chest - nuts   pop: Pop!   Pop!   Pop!   There's   a   Ives.

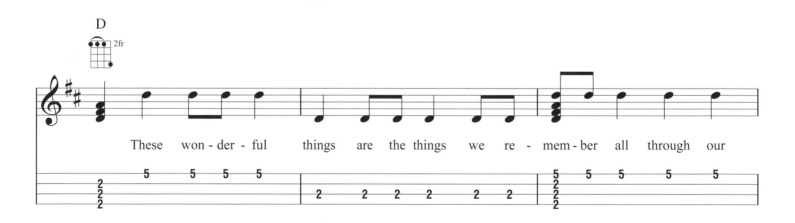

These   won - der - ful   things   are   the   things   we   re - mem - ber   all   through   our

D.S. al Coda 2
(take repeat)

Coda 2

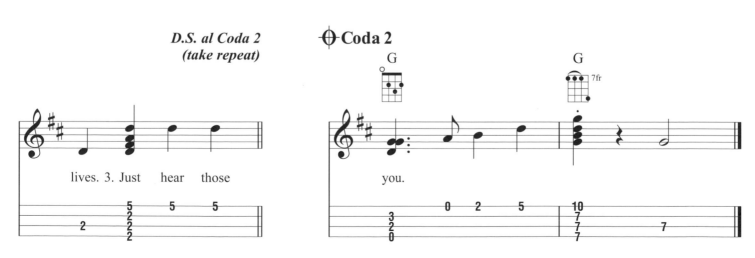

lives.   3.   Just   hear   those   you.

Sleigh Ride

Music by Leroy Anderson
Words by Mitchell Parish

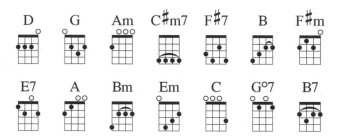

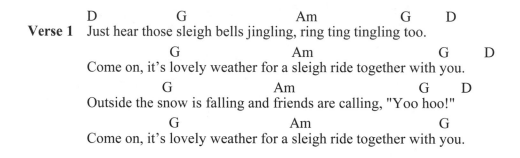

Verse 1

D   G   Am   G   D
Just hear those sleigh bells jingling, ring ting tingling too.
        G   Am   G   D
Come on, it's lovely weather for a sleigh ride together with you.
        G   Am   G   D
Outside the snow is falling and friends are calling, "Yoo hoo!"
        G   Am   G
Come on, it's lovely weather for a sleigh ride together with you.

Bridge 1

C#m7   F#7   B   C#m7
Giddy yap, giddy yap, giddy yap, let's go, let's look at the show.
        F#7   B
We're riding in a wonderland of snow.
        F#m   E7   A   D
Giddy yap, giddy yap, giddy yap, it's grand just holding your hand.

We're gliding along with a song of a wintery fairyland.

```
              D          G              Am           G     D
Verse 2   Our cheeks are nice and rosy and comfy cozy are we.
                        G              Am                    G      D
          We're snuggled up together like two birds of a feather would be.
                        G              Am           G     D
          Let's take that road before us and sing a chorus or two.
                        G              Am                         G
          Come on, it's lovely weather for a sleigh ride together with you.



                          D
Bridge 2  There's a birthday party at the home of Farmer Gray.
             Bm                        Em
          It'll be the perfect ending of a perfect day.
                 B              C     G°7    G   B7   Em
          We'll be singing the songs we love to sing without a single stop,
                 B              F♯7             B    D
          At the fireplace while we watch the chestnuts pop: Pop! Pop! Pop!

          There's a happy feeling nothing in the world can buy,
                  Bm                        Em
          When they pass around the coffee and the pumpkin pie.
                 B              C     G°7    G   B7   Em    D
          It'll nearly be like a picture print by Currier and Ives.

          These wonderful things are the things we remember all through our lives.



              D          G              Am           G     D
Verse 3   Just hear those sleigh bells jingling, ring ting tingling too.
                        G              Am                    G      D
          Come on, it's lovely weather for a sleigh ride together with you.
                        G              Am                 G     D
          Outside the snow is falling and friends are calling, "Yoo hoo!"
                        G              Am                         G
          Come on, it's lovely weather for a sleigh ride together with you.
```

What Child Is This?

Words by William C. Dix
16th Century English Melody

In 1865, an insurance company manager named William Chatterton Dix had a spiritual rebirth after recovering from a severe illness and a near-death experience. He began writing hymns. He set his poem "What Child Is This?" to the tune of a much older Elizabethan folk song, "Greensleeves," which goes back as far as 1580. Written in England, it has become popular in the United States and has joined the list of Christmas standards.

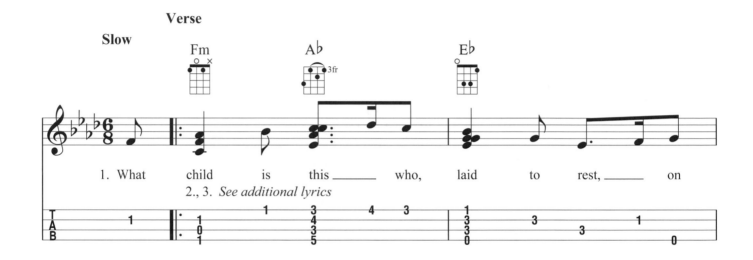

1. What child is this _____ who, laid to rest, _____ on
2., 3. *See additional lyrics*

Mar - y's lap _____ is sleep - ing? Whom an - gels greet _____ with

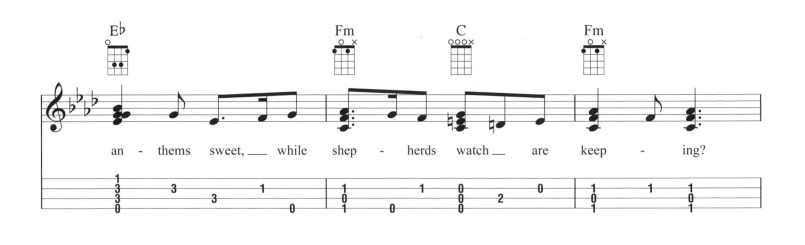

an - thems sweet, ___ while shep - herds watch ___ are keep - ing?

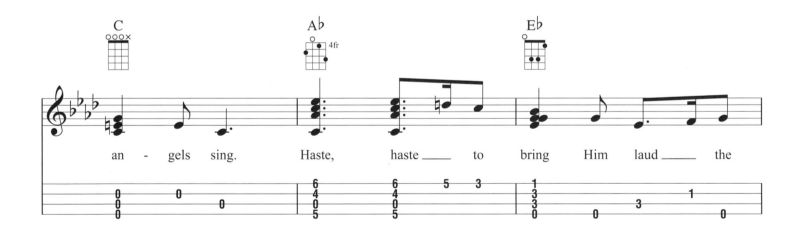

This, ___ this ___ is Christ the King, ___ whom shep - herds guard ___ and

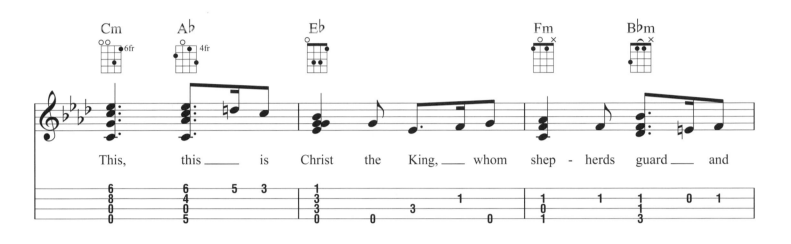

an - gels sing. Haste, haste ___ to bring Him laud ___ the

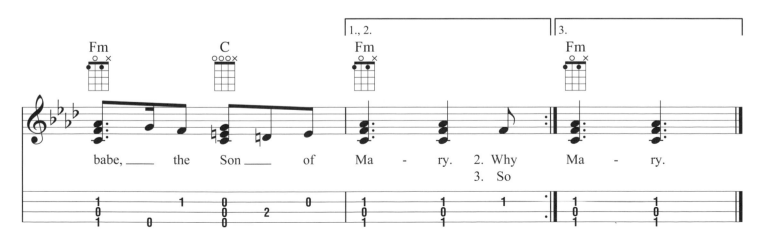

babe, ___ the Son ___ of Ma - ry. 2. Why Ma - ry.
3. So

What Child Is This?

Words by William C. Dix
16th Century English Melody

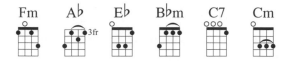

Fm   Ab   Eb   Bbm   C7   Cm

```
              Fm      Ab   Eb          Fm    Bbm  C7
Verse 1   What child is this, who, laid to rest, on Mary's lap is sleeping?
                Fm   Ab    Eb            Fm      C7      Fm
          Whom angels greet with anthems sweet, while shepherds watch are keeping?
          Cm  Ab   Eb            Fm      Bbm      C7
          This, this is Christ the King, whom shepherds guard and angels sing.
          Ab          Eb          Fm      C7      Fm
          Haste, haste to bring Him laud, the babe, the son of Mary.
```

```
              Fm     Ab   Eb           Fm    Bbm       C7
Verse 2   Why lies He in such mean estate where ox and donkeys are feeding?
                Fm      Ab    Eb        Fm  C7      Fm
          Good Christians, fear, for sinners here the silent word is pleading.
          Cm  Ab       Eb              Fm      Bbm  C7
          Nails, spears shall pierce Him through the cross He bore for me, for you.
          Ab          Eb              Fm      C7      Fm
          Hail, hail the word made flesh, the babe, the Son of Mary.
```

```
              Fm       Ab   Eb              Fm    Bbm   C7
Verse 3   So bring him incense, gold, and myrrh, come, peasant, king, to own Him.
                Fm   Ab    Eb          Fm  C7      Fm
          The King of kings salvation brings, let loving hearts enthrone Him.
          Cm  Ab   Eb              Fm  Bbm     C7
          Raise, raise a song on high, the virgin sings her lullaby.
          Ab          Eb              Fm  C7      Fm
          Joy, joy for Christ is born, the babe, the Son of Mary.
```

White Christmas

from the Motion Picture Irving Berlin's HOLIDAY INN
Words and Music by Irving Berlin

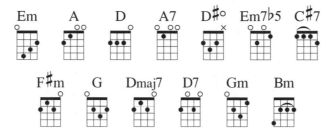

Intro-Verse

Em   A   D
The sun is shining, the grass is green,
    A7   D
The orange and palm trees sway.
D#° Em   A7   D D#° Em   A7   D
There's never been such a day   in Beverly Hills, L.A.
Em7♭5   A7   D
But it's December the twenty-fourth,
C#7   F#m Em A7
And I am longing to be up north.

Chorus 1

D   Em A7
I'm dreaming of a white Christmas,
G   A7   D A7
Just like the ones I used to know,
      D Dmaj7 D7   G   Gm
Where the tree-tops   glisten, and children listen
  F#m Bm   Em A7
To hear sleigh bells in the snow.

Chorus 2

D   Em A7
I'm dreaming of a white Christmas,
G   A7   D A7
With ev'ry Christmas card I write.
      D Dmaj7 D7   G   Gm
May your days be   merry and bright,
    F#m Bm Em   A7   D
And may all   your Christmases be white.

White Christmas

from the Motion Picture Irving Berlin's HOLIDAY INN
Words and Music by Irving Berlin

Bing Crosby's 1942 recording of "White Christmas" is said to be the world's best-selling single, having sold over 50 million copies to date. It may also be the "most covered by other artists" song of all time, though the Beatles' "Yesterday" may have upset that record. Irving Berlin wrote the tune for a 1942 film, *Holiday Inn*, which starred Crosby and Fred Astaire. Being aired on radio during World War II, the song, with its wistful, homesick message, was extremely popular and much requested by American soldiers overseas. Just after composing it, Berlin declared, "Not only is it the best song I ever wrote, it's the best song anybody ever wrote."

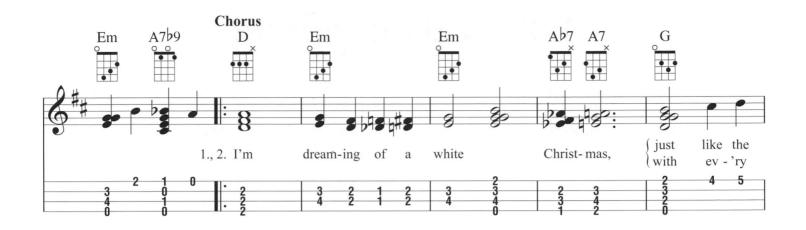

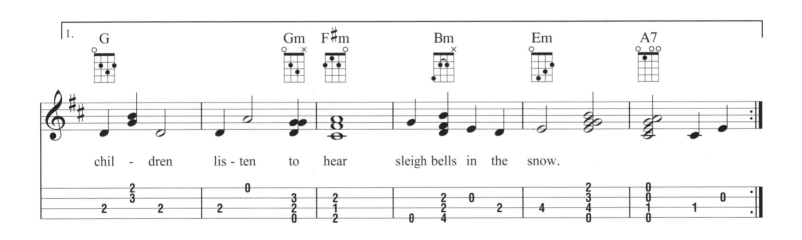

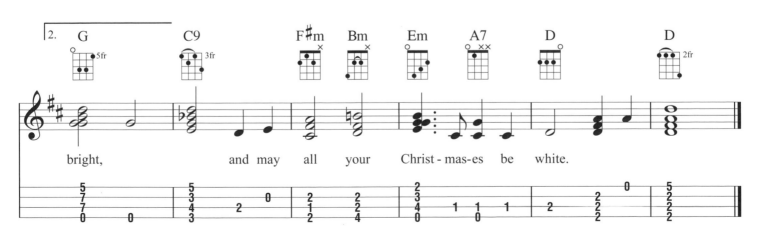

Winter Wonderland

Words by Dick Smith
Music by Felix Bernard

Richard B. Smith wrote the lyrics to "Winter Wonderland" in 1934, while being treated for tuberculosis. Composer Felix Bernard set it to music, and Guy Lombardo's chart-topping 1934 hit recording started the tune on its path to becoming a holiday standard. There are recorded versions by Bing Crosby, Michael Bublé, Snoop Dogg and Anna Kendrick, Dean Martin, Amy Grant, the Eurythmics, plus 200 other artists.

Winter Wonderland

Words by Dick Smith
Music by Felix Bernard

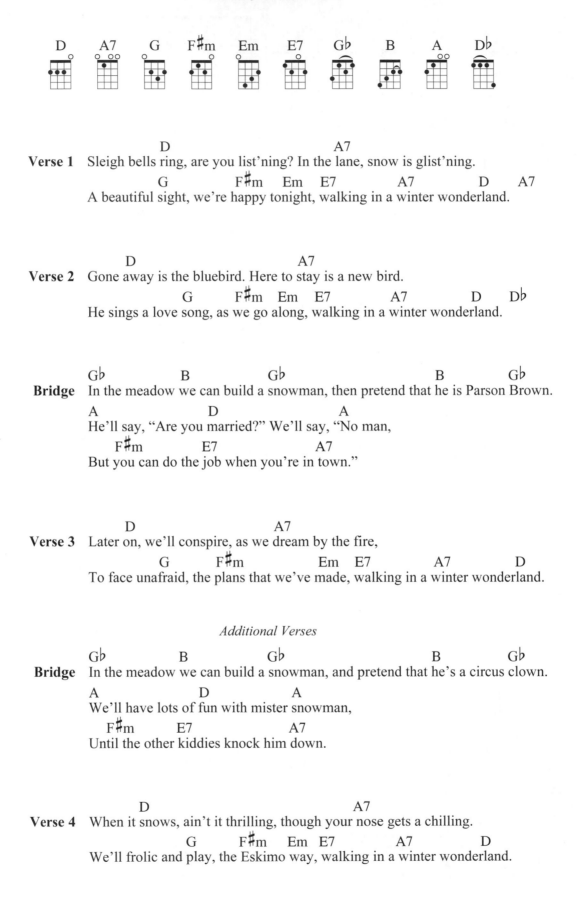

Verse 1
          D   A7
Sleigh bells ring, are you list'ning? In the lane, snow is glist'ning.
           G   F♯m Em E7   A7   D A7
A beautiful sight, we're happy tonight, walking in a winter wonderland.

Verse 2
          D   A7
Gone away is the bluebird. Here to stay is a new bird.
           G   F♯m Em E7   A7   D D♭
He sings a love song, as we go along, walking in a winter wonderland.

Bridge
G♭   B   G♭   B   G♭
In the meadow we can build a snowman, then pretend that he is Parson Brown.
A   D   A
He'll say, "Are you married?" We'll say, "No man,
  F♯m   E7   A7
But you can do the job when you're in town."

Verse 3
          D   A7
Later on, we'll conspire, as we dream by the fire,
           G   F♯m   Em E7   A7   D
To face unafraid, the plans that we've made, walking in a winter wonderland.

Additional Verses

Bridge
G♭   B   G♭   B   G♭
In the meadow we can build a snowman, and pretend that he's a circus clown.
A   D   A
We'll have lots of fun with mister snowman,
  F♯m   E7   A7
Until the other kiddies knock him down.

Verse 4
          D   A7
When it snows, ain't it thrilling, though your nose gets a chilling.
           G   F♯m Em E7   A7   D
We'll frolic and play, the Eskimo way, walking in a winter wonderland.

ABOUT THE AUTHOR

Fred Sokolow is best known as the author of nearly 200 instructional and transcription books and DVDs for ukulele, guitar, banjo, Dobro, mandolin, lap steel, and autoharp. Fred has long been a well-known West Coast multi-string performer and recording artist, particularly on the acoustic music scene. The diverse musical genres covered in his books and DVDs – along with several bluegrass, jazz, and rock CDs he has released—demonstrate his mastery of many musical styles. Whether he's strumming a Tin Pan Alley song on uke, playing Delta bottleneck blues, bluegrass or old-time banjo, '30s swing guitar, or screaming rock solos, he does it with authenticity and passion.

Fred's other ukulele books include:

- *101 Ukulele Tips*, book/soundfiles, Hal Leonard LLC
- *Beatles Fingerstyle Ukulele*, book, Hal Leonard LLC
- *Bluegrass Ukulele,* book/CD, Flea Market Music, distributed by Hal Leonard LLC
- *Blues Ukulele*, book/CD, Flea Market Music, distributed by Hal Leonard LLC
- *Fingerstyle Ukulele*, book/soundfiles, Hal Leonard LLC
- *Fretboard Roadmaps for Baritone Ukulele*, book/soundfiles, Hal Leonard LLC
- *Fretboard Roadmaps for Ukulele*, book/soundfiles (with Jim Beloff), Hal Leonard LLC
- *Hal Leonard Bass Ukulele Method*, book/soundfiles (with Lynn Sokolow), Hal Leonard LLC
- *Jazzing Up the Uke*, book/CD, Flea Market Music, distributed by Hal Leonard LLC
- *Ragtime Fingerstyle Ukulele*, book/soundfiles, Hal Leonard LLC
- *Slide and Slack Key Ukulele*, book/soundfiles, Hal Leonard LLC

Email Fred with any questions about this or his other guitar books at: **sokolowmusic.com**.

UKULELE NOTATION LEGEND

THE MUSICAL STAFF shows pitches and rhythms and is divided by bar lines into measures. Pitches are named after the first seven letters of the alphabet.

TABLATURE graphically represents the ukulele fingerboard. Each horizontal line represents a a string, and each number represents a fret.

2nd string, 3rd fret   1st & 2nd strings open, played together   open F chord

HALF-STEP BEND: Strike the note and bend up 1/2 step.

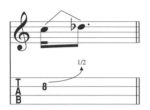

WHOLE-STEP BEND: Strike the note and bend up one step.

GRACE NOTE BEND: Strike the note and immediately bend up as indicated.

SLIGHT (MICROTONE) BEND: Strike the note and bend up 1/4 step.

BEND AND RELEASE: Strike the note and bend up as indicated, then release back to the original note. Only the first note is struck.

PRE-BEND: Bend the note as indicated, then strike it.

VIBRATO: The string is vibrated by rapidly bending and releasing the note with the fretting hand.

HAMMER-ON: Strike the first (lower) note with one finger, then sound the higher note (on the same string) with another finger by fretting it without picking.

PULL-OFF: Place both fingers on the notes to be sounded. Strike the first note and without picking, pull the finger off to sound the second (lower) note.

LEGATO SLIDE: Strike the first note and then slide the same fret-hand finger up or down to the second note. The second note is not struck.

SHIFT SLIDE: Same as legato slide, except the second note is struck.

TRILL: Very rapidly alternate between the notes indicated by continuously hammering on and pulling off.

TREMOLO PICKING: The note is picked as rapidly and continuously as possible.

NOTE: Tablature numbers in parentheses mean:

1. The note is being sustained over a system (note in standard notation is tied), or

2. The note is sustained, but a new articulation (such as a hammer-on, pull-off, slide or vibrato) begins, or

3. The note is a barely audible "ghost" note (note in standard notation is also in parentheses).

Additional Musical Definitions

(accent)   • Accentuate note (play it louder)

(staccato)   • Play the note short

D.S. al Coda   • Go back to the sign (𝄋), then play until the measure marked "***To Coda***," then skip to the section labelled "**Coda**."

D.C. al Fine   • Go back to the beginning of the song and play until the measure marked "***Fine***" (end).

N.C.   • No chord.

• Repeat measures between signs.

• When a repeated section has different endings, play the first ending only the first time and the second ending only the second time.

THE ULTIMATE COLLECTION OF
FAKE BOOKS

The Real Book – Sixth Edition
Hal Leonard proudly presents the first legitimate and legal editions of these books ever produced. These bestselling titles are mandatory for anyone who plays jazz! Over 400 songs, including: All By Myself • Dream a Little Dream of Me • God Bless the Child • Like Someone in Love • When I Fall in Love • and more.

00240221   Volume 1, C Instruments.....................$45.00
00240224   Volume 1, Bb Instruments....................$45.00
00240225   Volume 1, Eb Instruments....................$45.00
00240226   Volume 1, BC Instruments...................$45.00

**Go to halleonard.com
to view all *Real Books* available**

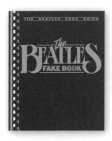

The Beatles Fake Book
200 of the Beatles' hits: All You Need Is Love • Blackbird • Can't Buy Me Love • Day Tripper • Eleanor Rigby • The Fool on the Hill • Hey Jude • In My Life • Let It Be • Michelle • Norwegian Wood (This Bird Has Flown) • Penny Lane • Revolution • She Loves You • Twist and Shout • With a Little Help from My Friends • Yesterday • and many more!
00240069 C Instruments...........$39.99

The Best Fake Book Ever
More than 1,000 songs from all styles of music: All My Loving • At the Hop • Cabaret • Dust in the Wind • Fever • Hello, Dolly • Hey Jude • King of the Road • Longer • Misty • Route 66 • Sentimental Journey • Somebody • Song Sung Blue • Spinning Wheel • Unchained Melody • We Will Rock You • What a Wonderful World • Wooly Bully • Y.M.C.A. • and more.

00290239 C Instruments......................$49.99
00240084 Eb Instruments....................$49.95

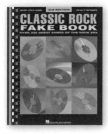

The Celtic Fake Book
Over 400 songs from Ireland, Scotland and Wales: Auld Lang Syne • Barbara Allen • Danny Boy • Finnegan's Wake • The Galway Piper • Irish Rover • Loch Lomond • Molly Malone • My Bonnie Lies Over the Ocean • My Wild Irish Rose • That's an Irish Lullaby • and more. Includes Gaelic lyrics where applicable and a pronunciation guide.
00240153 C Instruments...........$25.00

Classic Rock Fake Book
Over 250 of the best rock songs of all time: American Woman • Beast of Burden • Carry On Wayward Son • Dream On • Free Ride • Hurts So Good • I Shot the Sheriff • Layla • My Generation • Nights in White Satin • Owner of a Lonely Heart • Rhiannon • Roxanne • Summer of '69 • We Will Rock You • You Ain't Seen Nothin' Yet • and lots more!
00240108 C Instruments.....................$35.00

Classical Fake Book
This unprecedented, amazingly comprehensive reference includes over 850 classical themes and melodies for all classical music lovers. Includes everything from Renaissance music to Vivaldi and Mozart to Mendelssohn. Lyrics in the original language are included when appropriate.
00240044......................................$39.99

The Disney Fake Book
Even more Disney favorites, including: The Bare Necessities • Can You Feel the Love Tonight • Circle of Life • How Do You Know? • Let It Go • Part of Your World • Reflection • Some Day My Prince Will Come • When I See an Elephant Fly • You'll Be in My Heart • and many more.
00175311 C Instruments $34.99
Disney characters & artwork TM & © 2021 Disney

The Folksong Fake Book
Over 1,000 folksongs: Bury Me Not on the Lone Prairie • Clementine • The Erie Canal • Go, Tell It on the Mountain • Home on the Range • Kumbaya • Michael Row the Boat Ashore • Shenandoah • Simple Gifts • Swing Low, Sweet Chariot • When Johnny Comes Marching Home • Yankee Doodle • and many more.
00240151 ....$34.99

The Hal Leonard Real Jazz Standards Fake Book
Over 250 standards in easy-to-read authentic hand-written jazz engravings: Ain't Misbehavin' • Blue Skies • Crazy He Calls Me • Desafinado (Off Key) • Fever • How High the Moon • It Don't Mean a Thing (If It Ain't Got That Swing) • Lazy River • Mood Indigo • Old Devil Moon • Route 66 • Satin Doll • Witchcraft • and more.
00240161 C Instruments.....................$45.00

The Hymn Fake Book
Nearly 1,000 multi-denominational hymns perfect for church musicians or hobbyists: Amazing Grace • Christ the Lord Is Risen Today • For the Beauty of the Earth • It Is Well with My Soul • A Mighty Fortress Is Our God • O for a Thousand Tongues to Sing • Praise to the Lord, the Almighty • Take My Life and Let It Be • What a Friend We Have in Jesus • and hundreds more!
00240145 C Instruments.....................$29.99

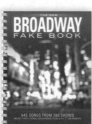

The New Broadway Fake Book
This amazing collection includes 645 songs from 285 shows: All I Ask of You • Any Dream Will Do • Close Every Door • Consider Yourself • Dancing Queen • Mack the Knife • Mamma Mia • Memory • The Phantom of the Opera • Popular • Strike up the Band • and more!
00138905 C Instruments............$45.00

The Praise & Worship Fake Book
Over 400 songs including: Amazing Grace (My Chains Are Gone) • Cornerstone • Everlasting God • Great Are You Lord • In Christ Alone • Mighty to Save • Open the Eyes of My Heart • Shine, Jesus, Shine • This Is Amazing Grace • and more.
00160838 C Instruments...........$39.99
00240324 Bb Instruments $34.99

Three Chord Songs Fake Book
200 classic and contemporary 3-chord tunes in melody/lyric/chord format: Ain't No Sunshine • Bang a Gong (Get It On) • Cold, Cold Heart • Don't Worry, Be Happy • Give Me One Reason • I Got You (I Feel Good) • Kiss • Me and Bobby McGee • Rock This Town • Werewolves of London • You Don't Mess Around with Jim • and more.
00240387.....................................$34.99

The Ultimate Christmas Fake Book
The 6th edition of this bestseller features over 270 traditional and contemporary Christmas hits: Have Yourself a Merry Little Christmas • I'll Be Home for Christmas O Come, All Ye Faithful (Adeste Fideles) • Santa Baby • Winter Wonderland • and more.
00147215 C Instruments $30.00

The Ultimate Country Fake Book
This book includes over 700 of your favorite country hits: Always on My Mind • Boot Scootin' Boogie • Crazy • Down at the Twist and Shout • Forever and Ever, Amen • Friends in Low Places • The Gambler • Jambalaya • King of the Road • Sixteen Tons • There's a Tear in My Beer • Your Cheatin' Heart • and hundreds more.
00240049 C Instruments.....................$49.99

The Ultimate Fake Book
Includes over 1,200 hits: Blue Skies • Body and Soul • Endless Love • Isn't It Romantic? • Memory • Mona Lisa • Moon River • Operator • Piano Man • Roxanne • Satin Doll • Shout • Small World • Smile • Speak Softly, Love • Strawberry Fields Forever • Tears in Heaven • Unforgettable • hundreds more!
00240024 C Instruments...........$55.00
00240026 Bb Instruments....................$49.95

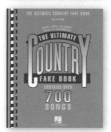

The Ultimate Jazz Fake Book
This must-own collection includes 635 songs spanning all jazz styles from more than 9 decades. Songs include: Maple Leaf Rag • Basin Street Blues • A Night in Tunisia • Lullaby of Birdland • The Girl from Ipanema • Bag's Groove • I Can't Get Started • All the Things You Are • and many more!
00240079 C Instruments...............$45.00
00240080 Bb Instruments $45.00
00240081 Eb Instruments $45.00

The Ultimate Rock Pop Fake Book
This amazing collection features nearly 550 rock and pop hits: American Pie • Bohemian Rhapsody • Born to Be Wild • Clocks • Dancing with Myself • Eye of the Tiger • Proud Mary • Rocket Man • Should I Stay or Should I Go • Total Eclipse of the Heart • Unchained Melody • When Doves Cry • Y.M.C.A. • You Raise Me Up • and more.
00240310 C Instruments............................$39.99

**Complete songlists available online at
www.HalLeonard.com**

The Best Collections for Ukulele

The Best Songs Ever

70 songs have now been arranged for ukulele. Includes: Always • Bohemian Rhapsody • Memory • My Favorite Things • Over the Rainbow • Piano Man • What a Wonderful World • Yesterday • You Raise Me Up • and more.

00282413 . . . . $17.99

Campfire Songs for Ukulele

30 favorites to sing as you roast marshmallows and strum your uke around the campfire. Includes: God Bless the U.S.A. • Hallelujah • The House of the Rising Sun • I Walk the Line • Puff the Magic Dragon • Wagon Wheel • You Are My Sunshine • and more.

00129170 . . . . . . $14.99

The Daily Ukulele

arr. Liz and Jim Beloff
Strum a different song everyday with easy arrangements of 365 of your favorite songs in one big songbook! Includes favorites by the Beatles, Beach Boys, and Bob Dylan, folk songs, pop songs, kids' songs, Christmas carols, and Broadway and Hollywood tunes, all with a spiral binding for ease of use.

00240356 Original Edition $39.99
00240681 Leap Year Edition $39.99
00119270 Portable Edition $37.50

Disney Hits for Ukulele

Play 23 of your favorite Disney songs on your ukulele. Includes: The Bare Necessities • Cruella De Vil • Do You Want to Build a Snowman? • Kiss the Girl • Lava • Let It Go • Once upon a Dream • A Whole New World • and more.

00151250 . . . . $16.99

Also available:

00291547 **Disney Fun Songs for Ukulele** . . . $16.99
00701708 **Disney Songs for Ukulele** $14.99
00334696 **First 50 Disney Songs on Ukulele** . $16.99

First 50 Songs You Should Play on Ukulele

An amazing collec-tion of 50 accessible, must-know favorites: Edelweiss • Hey, Soul Sister • I Walk the Line • I'm Yours • Imagine • Over the Rainbow • Peaceful Easy Feeling • The Rainbow Connection • Riptide • more.

00149250 . . . . $16.99

Also available:

00292082 **First 50 Melodies on Ukulele** . . . $15.99
00289029 **First 50 Songs on Solo Ukulele** . . $15.99
00347437 **First 50 Songs to Strum on Uke** . $16.99

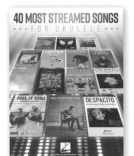

40 Most Streamed Songs for Ukulele

40 top hits that sound great on uke! Includes: Despacito • Feel It Still • Girls like You • Happier • Havana • High Hopes • The Middle • Perfect • 7 Rings • Shallow • Shape of You • Something Just like This • Stay • Sucker • Sunflower • Sweet but Psycho • Thank U, Next • There's Nothing Holdin' Me Back • Without Me • and more!

00298113 . . . . $17.99

The 4 Chord Songbook

With just 4 chords, you can play 50 hot songs on your ukulele! Songs include: Brown Eyed Girl • Do Wah Diddy Diddy • Hey Ya! • Ho Hey • Jessie's Girl • Let It Be • One Love • Stand by Me • Toes • With or Without You • and many more.

00142050 . . . . $16.99

Also available:

00141143 **The 3-Chord Songbook** $16.99

Pop Songs for Kids

30 easy pop favorites for kids to play on uke, including: Brave • Can't Stop the Feeling! • Feel It Still • Fight Song • Happy • Havana • House of Gold • How Far I'll Go • Let It Go • Remember Me (Ernesto de la Cruz) • Rewrite the Stars • Roar • Shake It Off • Story of My Life • What Makes You Beautiful • and more.

00284415 . . . . $16.99

Simple Songs for Ukulele

50 favorites for standard G-C-E-A ukulele tuning, including: All Along the Watchtower • Can't Help Falling in Love • Don't Worry, Be Happy • Ho Hey • I'm Yours • King of the Road • Sweet Home Alabama • You Are My Sunshine • and more.

00156815 . . . . $14.99

Also available:

00276644 **More Simple Songs for Ukulele** . $14.99

Top Hits of 2020

18 uke-friendly tunes of 2020 are featured in this collection of melody, lyric and chord arrangements in standard G-C-E-A tuning. Includes: Adore You (Harry Styles) • Before You Go (Lewis Capaldi) • Cardigan (Taylor Swift) • Daisies (Katy Perry) • I Dare You (Kelly Clarkson) • Level of Concern (twenty one pilots) • No Time to Die (Billie Eilish) • Rain on Me (Lady Gaga feat. Ariana Grande) • Say So (Doja Cat) • and more.

00355553 . . . . $14.99

Also available:

00302274 **Top Hits of 2019** $14.99

Ukulele: The Most Requested Songs

Strum & Sing Series
Cherry Lane Music
Nearly 50 favorites all expertly arranged for ukulele! Includes: Bubbly • Build Me Up, Buttercup • Cecilia • Georgia on My Mind • Kokomo • L-O-V-E • Your Body Is a Wonderland • and more.

02501453 . . . . $14.99

The Ultimate Ukulele Fake Book

Uke enthusiasts will love this giant, spiral-bound collection of over 400 songs for uke! Includes: Crazy • Dancing Queen • Downtown • Fields of Gold • Happy • Hey Jude • 7 Years • Summertime • Thinking Out Loud • Thriller • Wagon Wheel • and more.

00175500 9" x 12" Edition $45.00
00319997 5.5" x 8.5" Edition $39.99

HAL•LEONARD®
UKULELE
PLAY-ALONG

Now you can play your favorite songs on your uke with great-sounding backing tracks to help you sound like a bona fide pro! The audio also features playback tools so you can adjust the tempo without changing the pitch and loop challenging parts.

Ukulele Artist Songbooks

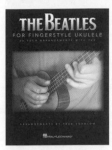

The Beatles for Fingerstyle Ukulele

arr. Fred Sokolow

25 favorite songs: Across the Universe • Can't Buy Me Love • Eight Days a Week • Here Comes the Sun • Hey Jude • Lucy in the Sky with Diamonds • Yesterday • You've Got to Hide Your Love Away • and more.
00124415 .... $19.99

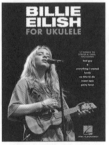

Billie Eilish for Ukulele

17 Eilish songs in standard G-C-E-A tuning for ukulele: Bad Guy • 8 • Everything I Wanted • Lovely • No Time to Die • Ocean Eyes • Party Favor • Wish You Were Gay • and more.
00345575 .... $15.99

The Doors for Ukulele

Now you can strum along to 15 Doors classics on the ukulele: Break on Through (To the Other Side) • Hello, I Love You • L.A. Woman • Light My Fire • Love Her Madly • People Are Strange • Riders on the Storm • Waiting for the Sun • more.
00345914 .... $14.99

Grateful Dead for Ukulele

Now Dead Heads can strum along to 20 of their favorites: Box of Rain • Brokedown Palace • Casey Jones • Friend of the Devil • The Golden Road • Ripple • Sugar Magnolia • Touch of Grey • Truckin' • Uncle John's Band • and more.
00139464 .... $14.99

Bob Marley for Ukulele

Ya mon! 20 Marley favorites: Buffalo Soldier • Could You Be Loved • Exodus • Get Up Stand Up • I Shot the Sheriff • Jamming • Lively Up Yourself • No Woman No Cry • One Love • Redemption Song • Stir It Up • Three Little Birds • and more.
00129925 .... $16.99

Best of Metallica for Ukulele

18 of Metallica's best arranged for uke: Enter Sandman • Fade to Black • For Whom the Bell Tolls • Master of Puppets • The Memory Remains • Nothing Else Matters • One • Ride the Lightning • Seek & Destroy • The Unforgiven • Until It Sleeps • Welcome Home (Sanitarium) • and more!
02502449 .... $22.99

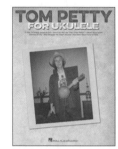

Tom Petty for Ukulele

17 Tom Petty tunes: American Girl • Don't Come Around Here No More • Don't Do Me Like That • Free Fallin' • Learning to Fly • Mary Jane's Last Dance • Runnin' Down a Dream • Wildflowers • You Don't Know How It Feels • more.
00192241 .... $15.99

Pink Floyd for Ukulele

15 unique arrangements especially for uke for Pink Floyd classics including: Another Brick in the Wall, Part 2 • Brain Damage • Breathe • Comfortably Numb • Have a Cigar • Hey You • Money • Time • Us and Them • Wish You Were Here • and more.
00128556 .... $14.99

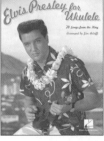

Elvis Presley for Ukulele

20 classic hits from The King, expertly arranged for ukulele by Jim Beloff. Includes: All Shook Up • Blue Suede Shoes • Can't Help Falling in Love • Heartbreak Hotel • Hound Dog • Jailhouse Rock • Love Me • Love Me Tender • Suspicious Minds • Teddy Bear • and more.
00701004 .... $16.99

Queen for Ukulele

14 hits from Freddie Mercury and crew for uke. Includes: Another One Bites the Dust • Bohemian Rhapsody • Crazy Little Thing Called Love • Don't Stop Me Now • I Want It All • I Want to Break Free • Killer Queen • Radio Ga Ga • Save Me • The Show Must Go On • Under Pressure • We Are the Champions • We Will Rock You • You're My Best Friend.
00218304 .... $15.99

Olivia Rodrigo – Sour

11 songs in standard GCEA uke tuning from Olivia Rodrigo's breakthrough debut album: Brutal • Deja Vu • Drivers License • Enough for You • Favorite Crime • Good 4 U • Happier • Hope Ur OK • Jealousy, Jealousy • 1 Step Forward, 3 Steps Back • Traitor.
00371695 .... $16.99

Jake Shimabukuro – Peace Love Ukulele

Deemed "the Hendrix of the ukulele," Hawaii native Jake Shimabukuro is a uke virtuoso whose music has revolutionized the world's perception of this tiny instrument. Songs include: Bohemian Rhapsody • Boy Meets Girl • Hallelujah • and more.
00702516 .... $19.99

Taylor Swift Ukulele Collection

Now Swifties can strum along to 27 songs on the uke: Blank Space • Cardigan • I Knew You Were Trouble • Love Story • Lover • Mean • Shake It Off • Today Was a Fairytale • Willow • You Belong with Me • and more.
00365317 .... $22.99